Envisioning Architecture

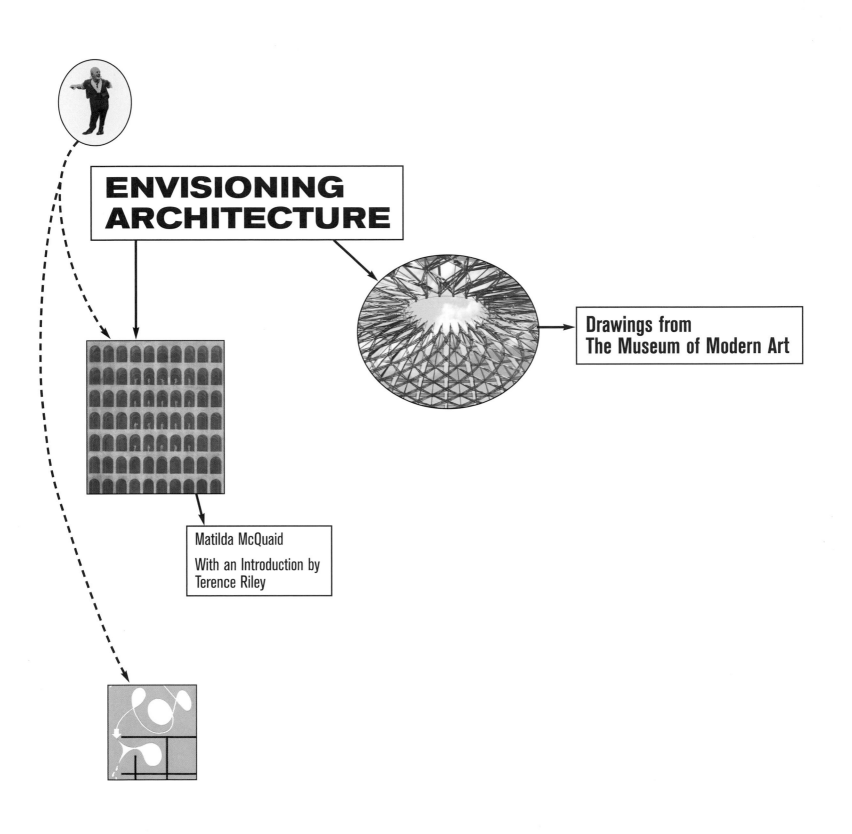

ENVISIONING ARCHITECTURE

Drawings from
The Museum of Modern Art

Matilda McQuaid

With an Introduction by
Terence Riley

The Museum of Modern Art, New York

Published on the occasion of **Envisioning Architecture: Drawings from The Museum of Modern Art**, an exhibition at the Royal Academy of Arts, London, December 7, 2002–February 16, 2003; the Schirn Kunsthalle, Frankfurt, April 29–August 3, 2003; and the Museu de Arte Contemporânea de Serralves, Porto, October 10–December 31, 2003

This publication is supported in part by a grant from the National Endowment for the Arts, and by Furthermore, a program of the J.M. Kaplan Fund.

Produced by the Department of Publications, The Museum of Modern Art, New York

Edited by David Frankel
Designed by Gina Rossi
Production by Christina Grillo
Printed and bound by Dr. Cantz'sche Druckerei, Ostfildern, Germany
Printed on 150 gsm LuxoOkay

Published by The Museum of Modern Art, 11 W. 53 Street, New York, New York 10019

Distributed outside the United States and Canada by Thames & Hudson Ltd, London

Library of Congress Control Number: 2002100732
ISBN 0-87070-011-1 (MoMA, Thames & Hudson)
ISBN 0-8109-6221-7

Printed in Germany

Cover: details of architectural drawings. Front cover, left, top to bottom: Bernard Tschumi; Hans Hollein; Ron Herron; Rem Koolhaas. Center: Otto Wagner; Ludwig Mies van der Rohe. Right: Frank Lloyd Wright; Aldo Rossi; Richard Neutra; Roberto Burle Marx. Back cover: Paul Nelson, Oscar Nitzchke, Frantz Jourdain; Ludwig Mies van der Rohe; Oscar Nitzchke. Title page, top to bottom: Albrecht Heubner; Chuck Hoberman; Ernesto Bruno La Padula; Herbert Bayer. Plate section opening, p. 39, left to right: O.M.A.; Ettore Sottsass; Erik Gunnar Asplund; Kisho Kurokawa

Contents

Foreword

*E*nvisioning Architecture: Drawings from the Museum of Modern Art is the first book in a three-volume series that The Museum of Modern Art is publishing on its collection of architecture and design. German editions of the books will be published by Prestel, Munich. Taken together the three volumes will provide a wide-ranging overview of the Museum's unparalleled collection of architectural drawings, design objects, and works of graphic design.

The Department of Architecture and Design was founded in 1932, three years after the founding of the Museum itself. The Department's first presentation was the seminal show *Modern Architecture: International Exhibition* (widely known as the "International Style" exhibition), organized by Philip Johnson, whose seventy-year relationship with the Museum extends from its earliest years to the present, and by Henry-Russell Hitchcock. The Department's collection was initially intended to be a study collection, containing only architectural photographs and models, but it soon expanded to include drawings, design objects, and graphic work. Drawings entered the collection in 1947, with the gift by Edgar Kaufmann, Jr., of Theo van Doesburg's *Contra-Construction* and the formal acquisition of two perspectival drawings by Le Corbusier for the Swiss Pavilion, Paris. The latter two had been exhibited in *Modern Architecture: International Exhibition*, and all three appear in *Envisioning Architecture*. Today the collection contains nearly 1,000 drawings, 179 models, as well as the Mies van der Rohe Archive of over 18,000 drawings and sketches. Throughout its history the collection has grown primarily through gifts from generous donors, including, most recently, the 205 visionary architectural drawings given to the Museum by The Howard Gilman Foundation. We have also benefited from the advice and stewardship of the members of The Museum of Modern Art Committee on Architecture and Design, whose distinguished chairmen have included Lily Auchincloss (1981–85), Marshall Cogan (1995–2001), and, today, Patricia Phelps de Cisneros.

The seventy-one architects represented in this volume range from the nineteenth-century Vienna architect Otto Wagner to the current deconstructivist Zaha M. Hadid, and include Frank Lloyd Wright, Ludwig Mies van der Rohe, Le Corbusier, Roberto Burle Marx, Oscar Niemeyer, Louis I. Kahn, and Hans Hollein, among others. Selected by Matilda McQuaid, former Associate Curator in the Department of Architecture and Design, the book's 144 plates celebrate both the breadth and the quality of the Museum's collection, as well as the richness and complexity of modern architecture as practiced over the course of the twentieth century. The works Ms. McQuaid has chosen reflect the diversity of architectural drawing, from carefully rendered plans and sections to abstract studies in form and space, from realized projects to imaginary ones never intended to be built, from theoretical projects that push the boundaries of architectural thinking to sensitive watercolors that explore the harmonics of space. Taken together these works offer a unique opportunity to examine architectural drawings of unparalleled beauty while documenting the most important trends in the history of modern architecture.

    This publication would not have been possible without the support and guidance of Terence Riley, Chief Curator in the Department of Architecture and Design. His essay on the history of collecting architectural drawings serves as the introduction to this volume. It is accompanied by an essay by Ms. McQuaid on the collection and exhibition of architectural drawings at the Museum over the last seventy years.

–Glenn D. Lowry
Director, The Museum of Modern Art

Acknowledgments

This publication has been made possible by a generous grant from the National Endowment for the Arts, with additional funding from Furthermore, a program of the J.M. Kaplan Fund.

The Museum's extraordinary collection of drawings would not exist without the architects who created them and the donors who made their acquisition possible. We have been the fortunate beneficiaries of great generosity in this regard. A particular debt is owed to The Museum of Modern Art Committee on Architecture and Design, which has been responsible for many acquisitions; led over the years by Philip Johnson, Lily Auchincloss, and Marshall Cogan, among others, and currently chaired by Patricia Phelps de Cisneros, it has been devoted to ensuring the collection's growth and strength. Equally important have been the Department's former directors, who, along with its curators, have given the collection its present shape. Since the establishment of the Department, in 1932, there have been only five directors: Philip Johnson, Philip Goodwin, Arthur Drexler, Stuart Wrede, and today Terence Riley. Each has produced an outstanding legacy of exhibitions and acquisitions.

Essential to this particular publication are not only the drawings themselves but their superb reproduction, the result of a 2 ½-year effort to produce digital images of the works in the Department's collection. This project was generously funded by the Andrew W. Mellon Foundation. The digital photography was coordinated by Luna Imaging, of Culver City, California, and I am grateful to Michael Ester, Maria Mapes, and Drake Zabriskie of that firm for their commitment to the project. Angelica Zander Rudenstine, Senior Advisor, Museums and Conservation, at the Mellon Foundation, was instrumental in providing funding and from the beginning believed in the importance of making this virtual collection available to a wide audience.

This publication accompanies a traveling exhibition. My gratitude goes to MaryAnne Stevens, Collections Secretary and Senior Curator at the Royal Academy of Arts, London, and to Max Hollein, Director, and Ingrid Pfeiffer, Curator, at the Schirn Kunsthalle, Frankfurt, who will be organizing the exhibition at their respective institutions.

At the Museum, Glenn D. Lowry, Director, has been an enthusiastic supporter of this project. Terence Riley, Chief Curator in the Department of Architecture and Design, provided not only valuable support during the book's preparation but also an insightful essay on the history of collecting architectural drawings. The Department of Imaging Services, under the leadership of Mikki Carpenter and assisted by Holly Boerner, has coordinated the photography with Luna, and Kate Keller, Head of Fine Arts Imaging, Erik Landsberg, Manager of Imaging Technology Development, and Jacek Marczewski, Fine Arts Photographer, have given valuable technical expertise all along the way. In the Department of Conservation, Karl Buchberg, Senior Conservator, and Erika Mosier, Associate Conservator, expertly prepared the drawings for photography and reviewed all of the drawing mediums for publication. In the Department of Development, Michael Margitich, Deputy Director; Rebecca Stokes, Director, Campaign and Development Communications; Elizabeth Burke, Associate Director of Development; and Preuit Hirsch, Senior Grants Officer, were instrumental in obtaining support from the Endowment, the Mellon Foundation, and the J.M. Kaplan Fund. Associate Librarian Jenny Tobias facilitated many aspects of the research, and Museum Archivist Michelle Elligott and Administrative Assistant Kathleen Tunney answered many spur-of-the-moment questions and helped in clarifying facets of the Museum's history. For the traveling exhibition my appreciation extends to Jennifer Russell, Deputy Director for Exhibitions and Collections Support; Ramona Bannayan, Director, Collections Management and Exhibition Registration; Maria De Marco Beardsley, Coordinator of Exhibitions; Randolph Black, Associate Coordinator of Exhibitions; Carlos Yepes, Assistant Coordinator of Exhibitions; Jerome Neuner, Director of Exhibition Design and Production; Peter Perez, Framing Conservator; and all of the staff in the Framing Department. For the book itself I am grateful to the staff of the Department of Publications: Michael Maegraith, Publisher; Harriet Schoenholz Bee, Editorial Director, always the best and most professional sounding board; Christina Grillo, Assistant Production Manager, whose patience and gentle pushing have kept the book on schedule; Gina Rossi, Senior Book Designer, who has crafted a beautiful publication that is a fitting tribute to the drawings; and Production Director Marc Sapir. It has been both an honor and a joy to work with Senior Editor David Frankel— his extraordinary patience, astuteness, and absolute professionalism have been the admiration of us all.

As always, the members of the Department of Architecture and Design have galvanized into creating this publication, and I would like to thank those who wrote for it: Paola Antonelli, Curator; Bevin Cline, Curatorial Assistant for Research and Collections, also a valued colleague in organizing the traveling exhibition; Tina di Carlo, Curatorial Assistant for Research and Collections, who has been so thorough in her attention to many last-minute details on the publication; Melanie Domino, former Cataloguer; Luisa Lorch, former Curatorial Assistant for Research and Collections, who tirelessly collated a mound of caption information; Peter Reed, Curator; and Terence Riley. In addition, Research Assistants Inés Katzenstein and Bryan Kessler compiled dossiers of information for each drawing that proved invaluable to all of the contributors. Pierre Adler, Steve Deo, Christian Larsen, Rachel Mayer, Nobi Nakanishi, and Curbie Oestreich have each played a significant role in taking up the slack in so many ways during this project. Finally I am eternally grateful to Craig Konyk, whose humor, intelligence, and support are my mainstay.

—Matilda McQuaid

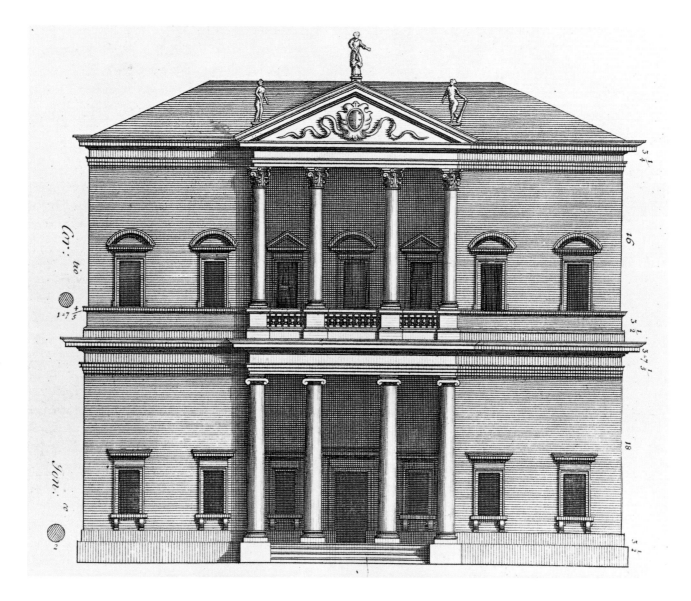

Drawn into a Collection: A Context of Practices

Terence Riley

Collections of architectural drawings today reflect a wide variety of cultural practices dating from as early as the fifteenth century. While these practices reflect the diverse intentions of innumerable individuals, the establishment of public collections of architectural drawings in libraries, museums, and archives reflects a specific point in what might be called the life of each individual drawing, a point at which these works have only arrived relatively recently.

At the time of its making, the drawing is part of a private process wherein an idea is given form. The frequent but always moving appearance of a draftsman's graphite fingerprint on a drawing is enough to recall the intimate relationship between the image and its maker. At another, later point, the same drawing may become a means of telling others how to construct a building. Then, at a more distant time, it may become part of a historical record, often revealing aspects of a project that are invisible in the building's working life. Together with other drawings, it may also become part of an even larger record of individual or collective achievement. In the great public collections that have been amassed over time, the individual drawing assumes the role of a basic element in constructing an idealized history with an implicit didactic mission. Indeed, the great collections of architectural drawings are the culmination of an almost inexorable trajectory from the private, the intimate, and the generative to the public, the expository, and, broadly speaking, the educational.

The history of architectural drawings is considerably shorter than the history of architecture. In the centuries before the Renaissance, only the most significant structures were "designed" (that is, their ultimate form was determined before construction began) using models and rough diagrams. Indeed, before the fifteenth century the essential skills and the basic material—paper—that would make drawing paramount in architectural and artistic practices were respectively yet to be discovered and not readily available. The invention of perspectival drawing by Filippo Brunelleschi in the early fifteenth century focused the interests of a great many *quattrocento* artists and architects, but it was the expanding availability of paper in the later part of the century that most enhanced the importance of drawing in the making of architecture as well as of painting and sculpture.[1] In the Renaissance, for the first time, architects and artists could accurately plan and depict a proposed building or work of art—in whole and in its parts—by mastering the skills of drafting and perspectival drawing. More important, drawing allowed the pursuit of the theoretical problems that would give the

Giacomo Leoni, after Andrea Palladio. Country House. 1716–21. Elevation. Copper etching, plate LXI from *The Architecture of A. Palladio, in Four Books*, 3rd ed., 1742, trans. of Palladio's *Quattro Libri dell'Architettura*, 1570

architecture of the Renaissance its defining characteristics: orderliness, a sense of scale, formal unity, and stylistic refinement.

Architectural models continued to play a role. Large-scale models were often kept at construction sites, where they were used to instruct the workers, rarely literate, who were to build the design. Models were also important in presenting both built and unbuilt architecture to patrons and the public, as they continue to be today; even four hundred years later, the first museum of architecture, which was established at the École des Beaux-Arts, Paris, in the early nineteenth century, displayed not drawings but full-scale plaster casts of architectural fragments, from the collection of Léon Dufourny, and a collection of cork models, assembled by François-Louis Cassas.[2] But casts and models of this type were replications of the results of the architect's designs rather than artifacts from their genesis and development. Meanwhile, the number of artists' and architects' drawings created as by-products, if you will, of the process of realizing buildings, as well as paintings and sculptures, had greatly increased by the end of the fifteenth century, as had the number of drawings generated by any one project.[3]

The Renaissance was the age of the rediscovery of classical architecture, and architects were fascinated by the precise and at times even mystical mathematical language of proportion, a language that could only be fully pursued through the use of sketches and measured drawings. Despite their status as preparatory studies or plans, architects' and artists' drawings came to be understood as important in their own right—as keys to understanding the formal and technical dimensions of a design—not long after they became a common part of artistic practice. As the initial works in which the architect or artist wrestled visibly with generative concepts, drawings also came to be seen as having an aesthetic and historical dimension almost rivaling that of the final product. By the late sixteenth century the critic and historian Giovanni Battista Armenini could confidently declare, "But for the colors," the preliminary drawing "is the work itself."[4] Giorgio Vasari similarly believed that the initial sketch was intrinsic to a work of art.[5] In 1550, he also noted the unique relationship between architecture and drawings: "Their chief use indeed is Architecture, because its designs are composed only of lines, which so far as the architect is concerned, are nothing else than the beginning and the end of his art, for all the rest, which is carried out with the aid of models of wood formed from the said lines, is merely the work of carvers and masons."[6] The earliest known instance of a preparatory work being accorded such value, according to the scholar Irving Lavin,[7] was in 1482, when Florence's Università dei Mercanti (Confraternity of merchants) decided to purchase the model for Andrea del Verrocchio's sculpture of Christ and St. Thomas, a work, set within an elaborate architectural niche, that they had commissioned for the church of Orsanmichele. The guild's reason for purchasing the model was quite like those of modern curators and collectors: they acted so that "the sketch and beginning of such a beautiful thing would not be spoiled or lost."[8]

Being concerned with "beautiful things," the private collectors of the sixteenth century, in addition to collecting artworks, might also, for example, have collected the architectural drawings of artists such as Michelangelo and Leonardo. The first systematic collectors of architectural drawings, however, were most likely architects themselves, who not only preserved their own drawings but also often collected each others'. Like the drawings of the painters and sculptors of the time, an architect's drawings became the intellectual and artistic capital of the atelier, a record of achievements as well as the basis for educating drafts-men and apprentices. Architects' recognition of the value—in terms of both pedagogy and, at times, commodity—of their drawing collections ensured that these archives would be passed on, not only to their descendants but often to their students. In the case of Leonardo, his architectural studies (as well as other drawings) were bequeathed at his death to his artistic heir and pupil Francesco Melzi. Likewise, it appears that the Renaissance architect Andrea Palladio left his drawings to his student Vincenzo Scamozzi. In an interesting twist, the Renaissance English architect Inigo Jones is believed to have bought Palladio's drawings from Scamozzi and subsequently to have left them to his own student John Webb. Webb in turn left them to his son William, with the proviso that they be kept together—a basic collector's impulse still recognizable today.[9]

While Vasari was not the first person to collect drawings, his efforts are notable for the extent to which they reflect the literary effort for which he is best known. *The Lives of the Artists* is the most popular rendition of the title of his influential book of 1550, but its full name—*The Lives of the Most Excellent Italian Architects, Painters, and Sculptors from Cimabue to Our Times*—gives more of a sense of his ambition. Vasari's book was the first chronicle of the protean artists who defined the birth, flowering, and maturation of Renaissance painting, sculpture, and architecture from the so-called proto-Renaissance of the early fourteenth century to his own time in the mid-sixteenth century. The breadth of Vasari's topic and the selectivity of his judgment were equally reflected in his collection, which ranged from sketches by Giotto, who died 200 years before Vasari was born, to works by more recent artists such as El Greco.[10] Vasari also collected sketches by architects, and his drawings by Donato Bramante, Brunelleschi, Francesco di Giorgio, Michelangelo, Palladio, Giuliano da Sangallo, Andrea Sansovino, and Scamozzi virtually constitute a capsule history of the best of Renaissance architecture. If artists' and architects' collections of their own drawings had a certain organic completeness, reflecting the way they grew from the maker's own artistic practices, Vasari's collection, like his book, aspired to being more synthetic than organic and more critical than complete. Both types of collection can be said to be "educational," but a further distinction might be drawn: artists' collections were used in "real time" to train the master's apprentices, while Vasari sought through his collecting and writing to educate a contemporary audience by constructing a historical framework.

The collecting practices of Inigo Jones reflected the sensibilities both of the Renaissance artists and architects and of Vasari, the connoisseur and historian who created a rich interplay among the works he acquired. Jones, like his professional forebears, not only retained the drawings produced by his own architectural practice but also collected contemporary drawings from English, French, Italian, and Flemish sources. What set him apart, however, was his collection of a great number of historical drawings, particularly sixteenth-century Italian works. Visiting Italy in 1613, Jones not only studied Palladio's buildings but also purchased the Italian architect's entire archive of drawings and prints, as well as a copy of his book *I Quattro Libri dell'Architettura* (Venice, 1570), in which Jones made copious notes. He also met with Scamozzi, one of Palladio's principal artistic heirs.

Whereas Vasari had collected drawings to create a history, Jones was collecting to create a present and ultimately a future. His studied familiarity with the works of Palladio transformed his own architecture from a self-taught native Gothic to the quick synthesis of his chosen master's work evident in the Banqueting House, London (1619–22), the Queen's House, Greenwich (1616–35), and other projects. While these works were enormously important among his peers, it is hard to imagine the spectacular rise of Palladianism throughout England and its far-flung colonies over the next two centuries without considering Jones's incredibly influential collection of drawings and books. His annotated copy of *I Quattro Libri* is preserved at Worcester College, Oxford, and several English translations were made of Palladio's book in the first half of the eighteenth century.[11] The rest of the collection he bequeathed to his student Webb, upon whose death it passed through a number of hands until purchased in 1720 by Lord Burlington, a passionate proponent of Palladianism who had engraved reproductions made of Palladio's and Jones's drawings and whose own country home, Chiswick, was modeled after Palladio's Villa Rotonda. At his death, Burlington left the collection of, by then, over 500 drawings—an amalgam of 250 works by Palladio, 116 by Jones, 108 by Webb, 27 by Burlington, and many others—to his heirs, who, in 1894, donated them to the Royal Institute of British Architects, London.[12]

The ever-increasing reproduction of architectural drawings by means of engraving, lithography, and various photographic processes from the sixteenth century onward would mean that with the passing of time there would be fewer instances of architects assembling large collections of original drawings by other architects as part of their practices. Libraries of books, and collections of photographs and later of slides, would become standard resources in architectural offices; many of these collections, like Jones's drawings, would eventually be given to professional and educational institutions. The best example of such a bequest might well be the books, drawings, and photographs of the American architect Henry Ogden Avery, who died prematurely in 1890 and whose collection was subsequently given by his father, Samuel, to Columbia University to establish the Avery Architectural and Fine Arts Library.[13] But architects have continued to archive their own drawings, and on a greatly expanded scale, particularly since the early twentieth century. The New York firm of McKim, Mead, and White, it can be argued, was the first "modern" architectural practice in that it adopted a corporate model, vastly altering the traditional "partnership" of architectural professionals. It was the largest and most prolific firm of its day, and its drawing archive consisted of 48,000 works—a quantitative increase in the number of documents an architectural firm might store, reflecting the increasing scale of modern construction. Even so, that figure remains a far cry from the volume of drawings generated by architects today. The contemporary firm of Skidmore, Owings & Merrill, founded in 1936, currently maintains approximately 350,000 drawings in its archives, which continues to grow at the rate of around 6,000 drawings per year.

Reflecting, perhaps, the increasing number of drawings in their holdings and the increasingly corporate nature of their practices, twentieth-century architects tended to bequeath their archives directly to professional societies, teaching and research institutions, and museums, rather than to individual students or associates. This custom actually began much earlier, one of the earliest examples being that of the British architect Sir John Soane, who began turning his London townhouse into a resource for students of the Royal Academy of Arts even before his death, in 1837. His 30,000-drawing archive, of not just his own projects but those of Robert Adam and Sir William Chambers, is still held there for the use of "amateurs and students," along with his expansive collection of plaster casts, models, and architectural and sculptural fragments. Examples of such bequests in the twentieth century include the gifts of the drawings of H. P. Berlage to the Bond van Nederlandse Architecten (Royal Institute of Dutch Architects) after the architect's death, in 1934, and of the McKim, Mead, and White drawing archive to the New-York Historical Society in 1950.[14] In 1976, friends and associates of Louis I. Kahn made arrangements for his archive to be acquired by the Commonwealth of Pennsylvania and placed on permanent loan to the University of Pennsylvania after his death. In other instances, institutions have been posthumously founded with the specific mission of maintaining an architect's archives for public study. Even before the death of Karl Friedrich Schinkel, in 1841, plans were made to establish a museum devoted to his work; his archive also included the drawings of his teacher and mentor Friedrich Gilly. This model later recurred in the establishment of such institutions as the Frank Lloyd Wright Archives (1961), the Fondation Le Corbusier (1968), and the Alvar Aalto Foundation (1969).[15]

A pair of lithographs by Le Corbusier, from 1932, of his design for the Swiss Pavilion at the Cité internationale universitaire, Paris, were the first drawings acquired by The Museum of Modern Art's Department of Architecture and Design. As such, they were the starting point for a collection that would combine aspects of both Vasari's and Jones's collecting practices. Just as Vasari had in his own time, the founding director of the Museum, Alfred H. Barr, Jr., believed that fundamental cultural changes had brought about a new art, distinct from everything preceding it, that needed to be documented and defined. Just as Vasari had constructed his historical narrative upon the work of Cimabue, Barr pointed to the work of the Post-Impressionist painter Paul Cézanne in developing his definition and history of modern art. Similarly, both Vasari's and Barr's collections reflected a critical depth rather than an encyclopedic breadth, Vasari concentrating on the "*più eccelenti*" artists and architects and Barr insisting on "the continuous, conscientious, resolute distinction of quality from mediocrity."[16] Barr, however, like Jones, had a vision of reorienting the culture of his time toward a new artistic paradigm. His historical narrative was to be the basis for understanding not only the art of his day but what he saw as the ever evolving future of modern art.

Encouraged by Barr, curators Henry-Russell Hitchcock and Philip Johnson sought to establish not only the historical development of architectural modernism but also its current position and its future course. Their landmark 1932 exhibition *Modern Architecture* (from which Le Corbusier's lithographs were acquired), commonly referred to as the "International Style" exhibition, did just that, referring both to sources from the past—the construction of the cast-iron-and-glass Crystal Palace of 1851, for example—and to recent turning points in what they saw as the simultaneous emergence of a new architectural sensibility in the work of Le Corbusier, J. J. P. Oud, and Walter Gropius around 1922. Hitchcock's and Johnson's efforts, the record shows, were clearly undertaken in the cause of Barr's zealous proselytization for all things modern, and their effect on the course of American and indeed global architecture was to be felt for the next four decades.[17]

The establishment of The Museum of Modern Art (which, interestingly, was chartered as an educational institution rather than a museum) thus represents both a transformation of existing collecting practices and radical innovations. As the first museum devoted to modern art, and as the first general fine-arts museum to have a curatorial department devoted to architecture, it became a model for institutions to follow, from the San Francisco Museum of Art (1935) to the Centre Georges Pompidou, Paris (1980). The once radical model of an architectural department can also seen in more focused institutions, such as the Archives d'architecture moderne, Brussels (1969), and the Archives d'architecture du XXe siècle at the Institut français d'architecture, Paris (1989).

The regulation of building activity by government agencies is part of the history of virtually every city in the world, and the archives of these regulatory agencies are no doubt the largest (albeit the least selective) network of repositories of architectural drawings in existence. Indeed the conservation of architectural drawings by the modern bureaucratic state has produced collections of architectural drawings on an unprecedented scale. The collections of architectural drawings in the U.S. Library of Congress (founded in 1800), Britain's National Monuments Record Centre (in Swindon, founded in 1908), and the Nederlands Documentatie Centrum voor de Bouwkunst (The Netherlands' National Documentation Centre for Architecture, founded in Amsterdam in 1970) were all established with the resources of the state, and their collections reflect their encyclopedic rather than critical foundations. Each of these institutions has holdings numbering in the millions of items.

The newest dimension to the collection of architectural drawings might be said to have two manifestations, the meta-collection and the cyber-collection. Both of these bring together preexisting collections of drawings, in the first case physically, in the second through the use of digital technologies. The meta-collection is typified by the holdings of the Netherlands Architecture Institute, Rotterdam (1988), which comprise numerous archives, from those of the Maatschappij tot Bevordering der Bouwkunst (Society for the Promotion of Architecture, 1842) to the National Documentation Centre for Architecture.[18] Similarly, the Cité de l'architecture et du patrimoine, scheduled to open in Paris in 2003, will subsume the Archives d'architecture du XXe siècle and other resources of the Institut français d'architecture and also of the Musée des monuments français.[19] By their very nature, these meta-collections are less ideological and more comprehensive in scope, seeking to give intellectual coherence and accessibility to a diverse group of documents previously pocketed within myriad private, institutional, and governmental archives. The same motivation can be seen in such efforts as ArtSTOR, an ambitious project of the Andrew W. Mellon Foundation that will bring together far-flung collections of art objects, including 750 architectural drawings from the collection of The Museum of Modern Art, in digital rather than physical form. Inherent in both the meta-collection and the cyber-collection is a previously unrealizable encyclopedic ideal.

While future technological developments cannot be predicted, the cyber-collection also appears to be the farthest reach of the trajectory from the intimacy of a drawing's creation to its dissemination as a collective educational resource for students and scholars alike. What is predictable, given centuries of precedent, is that new collecting practices will rarely replace preexisting ones—instead they will increase the overall scope of such practices. In this way, collections of architectural drawings such as those at The Museum of Modern Art will surely continue not only to grow but to grow in complexity. That complexity will grow in turn as part of an ever broadening and ever more accessible stream of information in the world beyond.

Notes

1. Europeans were importing paper from the Middle East as early as the tenth century, but apparently did not establish the craft of making it until the twelfth century, in Spain and Italy. In the fifteenth century the production of paper greatly increased as a result of developments in printing technologies.

2. In 1790–91, Guillaume Legrand and Jacques Molinos produced their design, never realized, for the conversion of the Palais du Louvre into a museum, which would have included the first public galleries for the presentation of architecture. The École des Beaux-Arts had become a depository for various collections of casts and fragments, and in 1813, on behalf of the school, the French state purchased François-Louis Cassas's models for the express purpose of creating a museum of architecture for students, professionals, and the public. For a detailed study of the conception of museums of architecture in postrevolutionary France, see Werner Szambien, *Les Projets de l'an II: Concours d'architecture de la période révolutionnaire* (Paris: École Nationale Supérieure des Beaux-Arts, 1986), and *Le Musée d'architecture* (Paris: Picard, 1988).

3. For a more detailed history see Carmen Bambach, *Drawing and Painting in the Italian Renaissance Workshop* (Cambridge: at the University Press, 1999).

4. Giovanni Battista Armenini, *Dé veri precetti della pittura* (Turin, 1586), Eng. trans. as *On the True Precepts of the Art of Painting*, trans. and ed. Edward J. Olszewski (New York: Burt Franklin and Co., 1977), p. 171.

5. "*Gli schizzi chiamiamo noi una prima sorte di designi, che si fanno per trovare il modo delle attitudine et il primo componimento dell'opera.*" Giorgio Vasari, *Le vite dé più eccelenti architetti, pittori, et scultori italiani, da Cimabue insino à tempi nostri. Nell'edizione per i tipi di Lorenzo Torrentino* (Florence, 1550), reprint ed. Luciano Bellosi and Aldo Rossi (Turin: Einaudi, 1986), p. 60.

6. Vasari, *Vasari on Technique: Being the Introduction to the Three Arts of Design, Architecture, Sculpture and Painting, Prefixed to the Lives of the Most Excellent Painters, Sculptors and Architects, by Giorgio Vasari*, trans. Louisa S. Maclehose (London: J. M. Dent, 1907), pp. 206–7.

7. Irving Lavin, "Bozzetti and Modelli: Notes on Sculptural Procedure from the Early Renaissance through Bernini," *Stil und Überlieferung in der Kunst des Abendlandes. Akten des 21. Internationalen Kongresses für Kunstgesichte* (Berlin: Verlag Gebr. Mann, 1967), pp. 111, 100.

8. Quoted in ibid.

9. See John Harris, *Catalogue of the Drawings Collection of the Royal Institute of British Architects: Inigo Jones and John Webb* (Farnborough: Gregg International Publishers, 1972), p. 7.

10. It is interesting to note that Vasari bound his drawings in elaborate albums, anticipating the publication of books with engraved reproductions of drawings, such as Palladio's *Quattro Libri*. After his death, unfortunately, his drawings were unbound and sold, and are now part of various far-flung collections. They are reconstituted, however, in Licia Ragghianti Collobi, *Il Libro de' disegni del Vasari* (Florence: Vallecchi, 1974).

11. *The Four Books of Architecture*, trans. Giacomo Leoni and Nicholas Dubois, 1715, and, the most popular, *The Four Books of Architecture*, trans. Isaac Ware, 1738.

12. See Prunella Fraser and John Harris, *A Catalogue of the Drawings of Inigo Jones (1753–1652), John Webb (1611–1672) and Richard Boyle, 3rd Earl of Burlington (1694–1753) in the Burlington-Devonshire Collection. With a History of the Burlington-Devonshire Collection & an Analysis of the English Drawings*, 1960, mimeograph typescript produced by the Sir Banister Fletcher Library, Royal Institute of British Architects, London.

13. The library was originally known as the Avery Architectural Library.

14. Sanford White's son, Lawrence Grant White, gave the bulk of the archive, and Mrs. James Kellum Smith, the widow of one of the later partners, donated a second, smaller group of drawings in 1968. McKim, Mead, and White's business records were given separately to the Avery Architectural and Fine Arts Library.

15. These dates represent different things. In 1961, Bruce Pfeiffer, now director of the Frank Lloyd Wright Archives, began the task of organizing Wright's drawings at the behest of the architect's widow, Olgivanna Wright. The Fondation Le Corbusier was founded posthumously in 1968 by decree of the French government. Alvar Aalto himself established his eponymous foundation, in 1969; after his death, the foundation bought his entire architectural archive from his heirs.

16. Alfred H. Barr, quoted in Philip C. Johnson, Preface, in Henry-Russell Hitchcock and Arthur Drexler, eds., *Built in USA: Post-war Architecture* (New York: The Museum of Modern Art, 1952), p. 8.

17. For more on Barr, Johnson and Hitchcock, and modern architecture, see my own study *The International Style: Exhibition 15 and The Museum of Modern Art* (New York: Rizzoli/CBA, 1992).

18. The National Documentation Centre for Architecture itself was constituted of several historical collections that at one time were separately maintained. See Mariet Willinge, "The Collection, Backbone of the NAI," *The Netherlands Architecture Institute* (Rotterdam: NAI Publishers, 1999), pp. 13–19.

19. On the Cité de l'architecture et du patrimoine see Jean-Louis Cohen, *Une Cité à Chaillot—Avant-première* (Besançon: Les Éditions de L'Imprimeur, 2001).

Acquiring Architecture: Building a Modern Collection

Matilda McQuaid

Architectural drawings are surrogates for concepts and for physical realities. Diverse in appearance and meaning, they can range from quick sketches capturing an essential design idea to computer-generated drawings whose realism leaves little to the imagination. Some drawings are autonomous acts, having no need for the actuality of architecture; others are more practical in purpose, as steps toward a built reality. Whether the ultimate outcome is some form of the preliminary idea or a complete departure from it, or even something finally unbuildable, however, the drawing serves the same end as the study or maquette in painting and sculpture: the development of an idea. What each drawing ultimately reveals is a discrete moment in the thought process and creative imagination of the architect.

The Museum of Modern Art has been collecting architectural drawings for almost seventy years, acquiring nearly 1,000 drawings by the most eminent architects of the twentieth century. (That number excludes the 18,000 drawings in the Mies van der Rohe Archive.) The achievements manifested in these drawings are integral to the development of modern architecture; they have also become bookmarks for events and periods in the history of the Museum's Department of Architecture and Design. Dramatic changes have occurred in the collection during these years, and one fundamental shift has been in the sense of the relevance of the architectural drawing. Once seen largely as documentary support material, these drawings have risen to the status of primary object and original work of art.

An equally important shift has come in the works' range of artistic expression: they have quickly broadened in the modern period to include everything from collages to computer renderings, reflecting not only the approach of the individual architect but the technological capabilities of the time. These changes were charted in the Department's exhibitions, especially after the 1960s, when original architectural drawings finally became an integral and significant part of the exhibition program. Exhibitions have played an essential role in the development of the architectural drawing's status as an important collectible. They have sometimes instigated collecting; conversely, they have sometimes followed on the coattails of specific acquisitions.

Although exhibiting and collecting generally have distinct outcomes, during the Department's first decade—it was founded in 1932—they were virtually the same, since the contents of every exhibition became part of the permanent collection.[1] This practice ended in the

Herbert Bayer. *Bauhaus 1919–1928*, The Museum of Modern Art, New York, December 7, 1938–January 30, 1939. Exhibition floor plan. Ink, gouache, and cut-and-pasted coated papers, 20³⁄₁₆ × 17¹³⁄₁₆" (51.3 × 45.2 cm). Purchase

1940s, but the Department's aim during its early years endured: "To foster good building in this country, and to collect and preserve records of good modern architecture throughout the world."[2] Sometimes this meant linking architects with potential clients, a popular activity of the Department's before World War II. In any case the concern was to maintain high standards of aesthetic quality, scholarship, and clarity in presenting this "important and sometimes difficult art to the public."[3]

The Museum's first architecture exhibition was *Modern Architecture: International Exhibition*, organized by Philip Johnson (the first chairman of the Department of Architecture) and Henry-Russell Hitchcock in 1932.[4] This exhibition, a major American showcase for modern architecture both here and abroad, included the work of nine architects, with an additional section devoted to the subject of housing. Comprising mainly models and photographs, it contained very few drawings, and the drawings it did accommodate were mostly floor plans or perspectives of projects unbuilt at the time (fig. 1). Immediately after the exhibition, seven out of its nine models were added to the collection, along with all of the photographs.[5] Two drawings by Le Corbusier for the Swiss Pavilion at the Cité internationale universitaire, Paris, which had been included in the show, were purchased directly from the architect, although they did not formally enter the collection until fifteen years later, when they would number among the Department's first official acquisitions of architectural drawings (p. 75; figs. 2–4).[6]

The Department's avid interest in models and photographs, and its early exclusion of drawings from the collection, reflected an attitude in which the building was seen as a work of art and the drawing as relatively insignificant, even though an integral part of the design process.[7] This was a striking departure from the established view of architectural drawings, which had been valued and collected for several centuries (see Terence Riley's Introduction, "Drawn into a Collection," pp. 10–17). Johnson, Hitchcock, and Alfred H. Barr, Jr., the Museum's founding director, seem to have felt uncertain about and even suspicious of unbuilt projects, whether these were experiments and visions—"paper archi-

1. *Modern Architecture: International Exhibition*, The Museum of Modern Art, New York, February 10–March 23, 1932. Installation view showing work by Frank Lloyd Wright

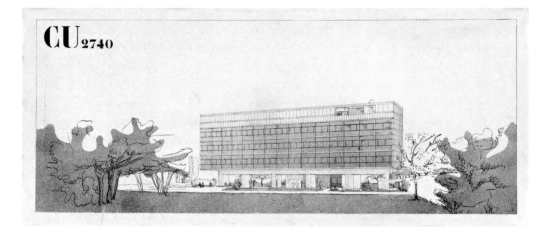

2. Le Corbusier (Charles-Édouard Jeanneret) and Pierre Jeanneret. Swiss Pavilion, Cité internationale universitaire de Paris. Perspective of south façade. Project: 1930–32. Drawing: 1932. Lithograph and airbrush on paper, 16 × 36⅞" (40.6 × 93.7 cm). Purchase

3. Le Corbusier (Charles-Édouard Jeanneret) and Pierre Jeanneret. Swiss Pavilion, Cité internationale universitaire de Paris. 1930–32. South elevation

4. Le Corbusier (Charles-Édouard Jeanneret) and Pierre Jeanneret. Swiss Pavilion, Cité internationale universitaire de Paris. 1930–32. North elevation

tecture"—or more definite plans that for one reason or another had gone unexecuted. The curators preferred realistic representations of built structures—demonstrations of possibilities that were inarguably within the reach of contemporary construction practices. Models and photographs performed that role, and photography, too, was in addition a specifically modern medium, making its use as a tool to describe another modern form appropriate and consistent.

The Museum's staff also saw their new institution as a populist one whose fundamental mission was to educate a general public about the developing culture of modernism. Models and photographs offered an innovative and extremely successful way to engage that audience: not only did they to some extent capture a building's three-dimensional materiality, they were often more immediately accessible than architectural drawings, which may well have technical aspects and functions that nonprofessional viewers consider barriers to interest and pleasure—particularly when the architectural forms themselves are unfamiliar and new. Much of the Museum's audience had most likely never experienced an exhibition of architecture, let alone of modern architecture. When the Department was conceived, no institution existed with a comparable mission of premiering the best of modern and contemporary building design. Johnson, in a report of 1932 titled "Need for a Department of Architecture," stated,

The Department of Architecture was founded . . . following the Exhibition of Modern Architecture held at the Museum. . . . Previously no organization existed for the exhibition of modern architecture. Contemporary architecture of all varieties was shown from a professional point of view semiprivately at the Architectural League, and from a commercial point of view at the Architectural League exhibition held every other year at Grand Central Palace. The Architectural League has taken no steps to inform the public of the most modern developments in contemporary architecture, perhaps because all its influential members were interested in either traditional styles or superficial, modernistic experiments.[8]

By the late 1930s the Department had organized over a dozen exhibitions, mostly dealing with contemporary work. These exhibitions were characterized by the relative insignificance of their attention to architectural drawings. The drawing was not considered precious in the same way as a painting or sculpture; it was a necessary stage in reaching the building finale, and it revealed the architect's design process, but it had not achieved the disembodied status of the singular object. Some architects did profess the absolute importance of the drawing: Eric Mendelsohn's statement "Look at my sketch, there is everything in it" made a direct link between drawing and built project.[9] Yet the Museum's 1941–42 exhibition *Architecture of Eric Mendelsohn* included only facsimiles of the architect's drawings. These were reproduced in actual size, and a label written by Mendelsohn explained their significance to him: "These sketches have no special captions, as their contours should clearly indicate their utility. For me they stand between the real and the abstract. Masses in motion tending to solve the absolute. Visions which could easily be changed to practical purpose."[10] Mendelsohn's actual drawings were not shown in the Museum, however, until nearly thirty years later, in the 1969 exhibition *Drawings by Eric Mendelsohn*.

The Department's exhibitions during that first decade of its history had an unfailing appeal to the public that can be attributed to a combination of factors: vivid presentation materials (models and photographs), new and modern subject matter, and the uniqueness of the art museum as a context for the study of architecture. In December 1938, shortly before the opening of the Museum's first permanent home, on 53rd Street, *Fortune* magazine published an article on its activities specifically commenting on the installation of one of its architecture exhibitions: the Museum had "perfected an informal and dramatic technique for exhibiting and explaining things in a way that makes people want to look at them, an example being a housing exhibition in 1934 in which the actual rooms, even to cockroaches, of an old-law New York tenement house were set up for comparison with a low-priced modern interior."[11] The article continued to laud the activities of the architecture department, which it depicted as one of the most successful in the Museum: "On the score of influence, the museum sees most concrete results from its work in architecture. . . . the department . . . has been one of the most important focuses of influence in making modern architecture increasingly interesting to the American public and noticeable in the American landscape."[12]

By this time the permanent collection included over 4,000 architectural photographs, compiled from exhibitions such as *Modern Architecture: International Exhibition*, *Early Modern Architecture: Chicago 1870–1910* (1933), *Architecture in Government Housing* (1936), *Modern Architecture in England* (1937), *Modern American Houses* (1938), and *A New House by Frank Lloyd Wright: "Fallingwater"* (1938). Although the photographs were transferred to a reference collection in 1941, their importance never diminished. During World War II, in fact, with Europe largely inaccessible to American architects and scholars, the Museum's photograph collection was a particularly valuable resource for material on European architecture.

It was not until 1947 that the Museum made its first official acquisition of three architectural drawings: Theo van Doesburg's *Contra-Construction* (p. 57) and Le Corbusier's two drawings for the Swiss Pavilion. Now the Department made a noticeable shift in the way drawings were thought about, exhibited, and collected, adopting a more synthetic approach across both mediums and departments. The Museum's Department of Painting and Sculpture had acquired its first van Doesburg canvas, *Rhythm of a Russian Dance* (1918), in 1946, and a painting by Le Corbusier, *Still Life* (1920), in 1934. The 1947 acquisitions added another dimension to the presence of these artists' oeuvres in the collection, and to the Museum's collecting practice.

A change in the visual experience of architecture exhibitions began that same year, with *Mies van der Rohe*, designed by the architect himself (figs. 5 and 6). The show contained only a few actual drawings (most of Mies's drawings from his Berlin years, in any case, were

5–6. *Mies van der Rohe*, The Museum of Modern Art, New York, September 16, 1947–January 25, 1948. Installation views. 5: photomural of the Friedrichstrasse Skyscraper Project (left). 6: photomural of the Monument to the November Revolution (left)

still in Germany, and were inaccessible for years after the war), but there were mural-scale photographic reproductions of both drawings and buildings, which engaged the viewer and in some cases suggested the illusion of actually entering one of the architect's spaces.[13] The most famous of Mies's German designs, the Friedrichstrasse Skyscraper Project (1921; p. 51), was represented through a photomural larger than the drawing it showed, so that the building seemed to soar upward and over the visitor, surely becoming more effective in this sense than in the original. Mies also included collages in the exhibition, but these were not working drawings; they were created for the occasion, and were seen as "explanatory material," as noted in the caption for one of the publicity photographs of the installation in the Museum's files. The label also mentioned some of the most pertinent issues related to the display of architecture: "The exhibition of architecture, an important part of the museum's undertaking, presents one of its most complex problems: scale, outdoor ambience, comprehensibility for the layman and at the same time technical detail for the student. Here we have a photo mural on the left, a model on the pedestal and plans and explanatory material on the walls, as well as chairs designed by the architect."[14] In many ways this combination of elements represented an ideal in the Museum's evolving approach to architectural exhibitions, the varied contents creating an environment that was easy to experience and digest. The emphasis was more on the feeling of the project or building than on a complete visual representation of it.

An exhibition in 1951, *Le Corbusier: Architecture, Painting, Design*, included works in all of the fields named in the title (figs. 7 and 8). The curator was Arthur Drexler, who would become director of the Department of Architecture and Design in 1955. Like Barr, Drexler cherished the idea of a collection that went beyond painting and sculpture to include

architecture, design, film, and photography. He integrated several of these in his Le Corbusier show, arguing,

> By comparing Le Corbusier's work in these three different fields, some of the characteristics of his decisive contribution to modern art become very clear. The earliest work shown, the painting "Deux Bouteilles," done in 1926, illustrates his preoccupation with a geometrically established system of proportions and subdued, closely related color. The architectural forms of the Villa Savoye are developed with a painter's feeling for color and space. . . . The reclining chair is a plane surface bent to shape and supported on a sculptured base,

while the leather lounge chair is itself a piece of sculpture balanced on slender metal columns, recalling the Villa Savoye. The perspective drawing of proposed glass skyscrapers in Paris, done in 1930, is remarkable for its pictorially romantic qualities, suggesting an attitude that is as much a part of the painter's approach as it is of the architect's.[15]

The perspective drawing itself, however, was not included in the exhibition; instead a six-foot-high photo-enlargement of it seemed to invite the viewer into Le Corbusier's visionary town-planning concept of the "Radiant City." It was not until 1978 that this architect's drawings were shown in any depth, but that year they received an entire exhibition, *Le Corbusier: Architectural Drawings*.

By 1952, Museum records show, there were sixty original architectural drawings in the collection, as well as fourteen models. Only five drawings have acceptance dates before 1952, however; the remaining fifty-five were most likely on extended loan from Mies, in a group that was finally acquired in 1963. It is interesting to note that until this large Mies acquisition, the majority of the Department's drawings were not by architects but by figures such as van Doesburg who had other artistic interests. Between 1948 and 1954, for example, the Department acquired three gouaches by the Brazilian painter and landscape designer Roberto Burle Marx. One of these colorful and abstract renderings was included in the 1949 exhibition *From Le Corbusier to Niemeyer: 1929–1949* (directed by Johnson with Hitchcock as consultant), which aimed to show the widespread influence of Le Corbusier by featuring his Villa Savoye (1929–31) alongside other works including Oscar Niemeyer's Beach House Project for Mr. and Mrs. Burton Tremaine (1948; pp. 104–5).[16] Burle Marx had designed the garden for the Tremaine house, and his gouache was exhibited next to Jean Arp's wooden *Relief* (1938–39), also owned by the Museum (fig. 9). The juxtaposition was appropriate in terms of the two works' formal similarities, and Arp had been influential for Burle Marx. More important, though,

9. *From Le Corbusier to Niemeyer: 1929–1949*, The Museum of Modern Art, New York, February 15–April 3, 1949. Installation view showing Jean Arp's *Relief* (left) and Roberto Burle Marx's *Garden Design* (right)

was the artistic dimension of Burle Marx's drawings, as opposed to their function as architectural plans. A wall label remarked,

> The new Brazilian gardens designed by the painter Roberto Burle Marx carry the free-form, fantastic tradition of Arp and Miró into direct contact with architecture. They are, of course, less "psychological" than the painting and sculpture in this style, since they must approach the utilitarian. They seem, however, to be as direct a translation of nonmechanical abstract painting into gardening terms as the English parks of the eighteenth century were of the classical landscape painting of Poussin and Claude.[17]

Frederick Kiesler, whose drawings were shown in the 1952 exhibition *Two Houses: New Ways to Build*, was another architect who was equally well known for his work in other fields, in his case those of sculpture and stage design. The exhibition, organized by Drexler, juxtaposed drawings and a model of Kiesler's Endless House with a model of Buckminster Fuller's Geodesic Dome, the two structures serving as examples of different approaches producing similarly nonorthogonal architectural spaces. Kiesler's approach was characterized as "aesthetic," Fuller's as more scientific. After seeing the exhibition, Kiesler admonished Drexler for this categorization:

> While I appreciate your idea of juxtaposing my model and drawings with that of Fuller's, his being conceived from a mechanistic point of view while mine from an esthetic one, I cannot agree with you regarding my own house. I can only state the fact that it has primarily been conceived for the creation of satisfactory living conditions, the spatial areas needed for this purpose, and that from these conditions I had arrived at the dimensions, the form and the construction scheme. The esthetic aspect comes with it and was not the primary thought.[18]

The Museum had acquired several pieces of Kiesler's furniture from Peggy Guggenheim's Art of This Century Gallery in 1948, four years earlier; around the time of the exhibition it purchased all of Kiesler's drawings for his Endless House Project (pp. 108–9), but did not formally acquire them until 1966.

In the Museum's first decades it had only one acquisitions committee, the Committee on Museum Collections, which acquired works of every kind. In October 1967 that arrangement ended and separate committees were formed for each of the five, medium-specific curatorial departments that the Museum then maintained.[19] The catholic nature of the pre-1967 committee may help to explain not only its interest in Kiesler, Burle Marx, and others whose work translated across various departmental specialties but also its relative slowness in acquiring architectural drawings, whose visual merit may not always have been self-evident to curators more committed to other branches of the arts. An acquisitions committee dedicated to architecture and design was surely more likely to pursue architectural drawing than a committee on which architecture curators were a minority.

The exhibitions and acquisitions programs now made no hierarchical distinctions between built and unbuilt projects; the architect's idea was the focus whether it had been realized at full

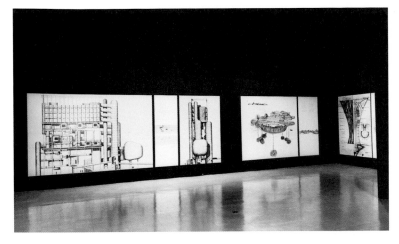

10–12. *Visionary Architecture*, The Museum of Modern Art, New York, September 29–December 4, 1960. Installation views. 10 (top left): Michael Webb's Furniture Manufacturers Association Headquarters Project (two photomurals on left) and William Katavolos's Chemical Architecture Project (two photomurals on right). 11 (top right): photomurals of Paolo Soleri's Biotechnic City, Buckminster Fuller's Partial Enclosure of Manhattan Island, Louis Kahn's Civic Center, and Kahn's City Tower projects. 12 (bottom), left to right: Frederick Kiesler's place de la Concorde Project drawing, three drawings of Kiesler's Endless Theater Project, photomural of Kiesler's Endless House Project, and model of Kiesler's Endless House Project

scale or existed only on paper. But the Museum's curators apparently felt that where photographic documentation of an existing building was an impossibility, the most expedient way to transmit that idea in exhibitions was to create the sense of a whole environment. The projects in the *Visionary Architecture* exhibition of 1960, for example, were represented primarily by models and photographs, and when Drexler, once again the exhibition's curator, did turn to drawings, he mostly showed them in reproduction and at a large scale (figs. 10–12). As in the 1947 Mies exhibition, viewers were made to feel as if they were entering another world. The grand scale of these photo-enlargements created an extraordinary environment that was accessible to the museum visitor. One of the few architects represented by actual drawings was Kiesler, whose depictions of his Endless Theater and place de la Concorde projects were already very large, measuring over six feet wide (fig. 13). (The Museum would acquire these drawings in 1966, at the same time that it formally acquired the drawings of Kiesler's Endless House that had long been in its possession.) Louis Kahn's eleven-by-fourteen-inch sketch for his Civic Center Project (p. 114), on the other hand, which the Museum would acquire four years later, was reproduced at many times its original size, transformed from an architect's ideal to a life-size visage of a city.[20]

In an introduction to the exhibition, Drexler wrote,

The history of architecture includes many great projects never intended to be built. There is indeed a "paper" architecture unhampered by technical details, uncompromised by the whims of patrons, and freed from the exigencies of finance, politics, and custom. Such visionary projects afford the architect an opportunity to rebuild the world as he knows it ought to be, and it is the world that the architect—visionary or otherwise—really wishes to change.[21]

Implicit in this argument was a recognition of the value of the drawing, and, whether coincidentally or not, the Museum began to collect architectural drawings seriously not long after

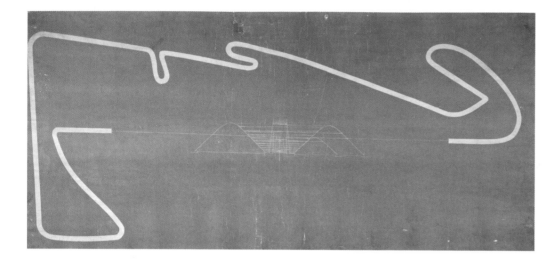

the *Visionary Architecture* exhibition. In a sense it had rediscovered the architectural drawing's elsewhere well-established role as a singular object with an existence independent of three-dimensional realization. The Department's exhibitions had given it a growing familiarity with the medium, paving the way for aggressive collecting; at the same time, it had developed a profound respect for the intrinsic beauty of architectural drawings, which it openly expressed in its first exhibition exclusively devoted to them, *Frank Lloyd Wright Drawings* of 1962 (fig. 14).

The exhibition contained 250 drawings, all of them selected from the collection of 8,000 at the Taliesin Archives in Taliesin, Wisconsin. The exhibition was organized by Drexler and Wilder Green, the Department's assistant director, with Green selecting and installing the works and Drexler making the final selection and writing the text for the publication. In a letter to William Wesley Peters, Wright's son-in-law and chief architect in the firm of Taliesin Associated Architects at Taliesin West in Scottsdale, Arizona, Drexler wrote,

> *I am delighted that you're able to accept our offer of an exhibition of Frank Lloyd Wright drawings. Indeed, I cannot tell you how satisfying this is to me personally: Mr. Wright's drawings are among the most beautiful architectural studies ever made and I can think of no better way of reaffirming his stature as an artist than by making them visible to the public. . . . I believe the drawings should be presented as works of art rather than as part of a documentation of actual or projected buildings. For this reason it seems preferable to omit architectural models. On the other hand, it might be helpful to include small photographs of completed buildings taken from points of view comparable to those of the drawings, but only when such photographs would be relevant to an appreciation of the drawings themselves.[22]*

Drawings, clearly, were finally being seen as works of art. In addition, of course, they often surpassed the built form of the project in demonstrating the development of the design; in his introduction to the book, Drexler writes that however beautiful the drawings are, they cannot be separated from the thought and feeling that made them so—indeed "the drawings sometimes tell us more about Wright's thought than is apparent in the finished

14. *Frank Lloyd Wright Drawings.* The Museum of Modern Art, New York, March 14–May 6, 1962. Installation view

buildings."[23] They are visual statements of Wright's thought process. But although drawings like these had been presented in exhibitions before (if mostly in facsimile form), they were now judged not only by the ideas they stood for but also by the beauty of their draftsmanship and composition. One reviewer of the exhibition commented specifically on the book's refusal to crop any of the images:

> *Each Wright drawing is of itself a work of art, and is presented in this book as a painting is best shown: as a thing entire, uncropped to the four edges of the space within which it was composed. Viewing each drawing as a whole makes it possible to see more clearly the influence of Japanese art upon Wright's draftsmanship. Buildings seen from below are frequently placed at the top of the sheet and empty surfaces of paper are used to convey distance.*[24]

The Museum acquired no drawings directly from the exhibition, but acquired a set of lithographs for Wright's American System-Built Houses (pp. 44–45) over thirty years later, around the time of the 1994 Wright exhibition curated by Riley with Peter Reed. In 1999, other drawings shown in the 1962 exhibition—for Unity Temple (p. 43) and St. Mark's-in-the-Bouwerie Towers (p. 55)—were also acquired, and reunited at the Museum as parts of the permanent collection.

In 1963 the Department acquired sixty-five drawings by Mies, along with works by Walter Pichler and Hans Hollein. In 1964 it gained its first collection galleries, in which over 200 works of architecture and design could be presented at any one time, and two years later it organized its first major collection show of drawings, *Ludwig Mies van der Rohe: Drawings in*

the Collection of The Museum of Modern Art. The exhibition, which contained seventy-eight works, was extremely significant in demonstrating the Department's commitment to the presentation of Mies's architecture, and so in securing the subsequent acquisition, in 1968, of an archive of drawings by one of the twentieth century's foremost architects. One of the motivations behind the show, in fact, was to generate an inventory of the drawings still in Mies's possession, and which he had promised to the Museum. Almost twenty years earlier, in 1947, the Friedrichstrasse Skyscraper drawing had been represented in the form of a photomural in the first Mies exhibition; now it was exhibited in its original form (fig. 15). One has only to compare this drawing with the model of the Friedrichstrasse Skyscraper (fig. 16) to understand Drexler's comment, "Some of these drawings are among the most compelling architectural images ever made, and they reveal even more clearly than do photographs of actual buildings the development of Mies's ideas about structure and space."[25]

Only a year later, in 1967, another collection exhibition opened, *Architectural Fantasies: Drawings from the Museum's Collection* (fig. 17).[26] Curated by Drexler, the show contained works by the architects Hollein and Raimund Abraham and by the sculptor Pichler. Continuing in the vein of the 1960 show *Visionary Architecture* but focusing on current work, *Architectural Fantasies* proceeded from a sense of the inadequacy of inherited forms, even "modern" ones, to speculate on architecture's future. Fascinated by the complexity and scale of contemporary machinery, Hollein (pp. 136–37, 146–49), Abraham (pp. 140–41), and Pichler (p. 139) imagined architectures actually made out of machines, as opposed to merely incorporating them, as Le Corbusier had envisioned.

17. *Architectural Fantasies: Drawings from the Museum's Collection*, The Museum of Modern Art, New York, July 27, 1967–February 12, 1968. Installation view, including Hans Hollein's Aircraft Carrier City in Landscape Project

18. *The Architecture of the Ecole des Beaux-Arts*, The Museum of Modern Art, New York, October 29, 1975–January 4, 1976. Installation view

Exhibitions did not always lead to acquisitions; just as often, in fact, an acquisition preceded an exhibition. The Department, for example, acquired approximately thirty-seven drawings of Kahn's in 1964, two years before organizing its first comprehensive review of his work. Superstudio's *First City* (1971; p. 162) and Friedrich St. Florian's *New York Birdcage–Imaginary Architecture Project* (1968; p. 155) were not acquired from an exhibition but were collected independently, in part because of their continuation of the themes of the *Visionary Architecture* exhibition. Acquisitions such as these led in turn to the recent large gift of over 200 visionary drawings from The Howard Gilman Foundation. This kind of mirroring between collecting and exhibiting has succeeded in creating a personal and somewhat idiosyncratic collection.

As the Department's exhibitions generally began to include more drawings, and as drawings became the specific subject of more of the Department's exhibitions, the collecting effort came to focus not only on works of great architecture but on drawings that were themselves great expressive achievements. The *Frank Lloyd Wright Drawings* exhibition of 1962 had been the first to stress the beauty of architectural drawing as a form. Thirteen years later, *The Architecture of the Ecole des Beaux-Arts* (1975–76) reiterated this sentiment, and if the Wright exhibition had commemorated the extraordinary talent of a single architect in the drawing medium, an underlying purpose of the later show was to celebrate the art of drawing itself (fig. 18). Arguing that the architectural drawing "makes the act of drawing substitute for the real condition of a proposed architectural form,"[27] Drexler, the exhibition's curator, presented beautiful renderings from the mid-nineteenth and early twentieth centuries by former students of the Ecole. Part of his intention was to show the influence of such works on certain American pioneers of modern architecture, like H. H. Richardson and Louis Sullivan, but the exhibition was also meant to influence the current practice of architectural presentation. In a wall label Drexler explained,

Social and cultural developments, politics, economics, and technology determine what will be built; the manner in which architecture is taught determines how it will be built. In the present stage of modern architecture's evolution, a mode of conceptualizing buildings through models has so far replaced drawing that students are likely to think in terms of designing and constructing a model, rather than an actual building. Conceptualizing architecture through drawings has been all but abandoned. Drawing, like model making, can become an end in itself and serve to distract attention from real problems. But at its best it is an instrument of thought that is at once precise and far-ranging; and it can encourage infinitely subtle perceptions of built form.[28]

Drexler's next exhibition, *Le Corbusier: Architectural Drawings* (1978), recalled the Beaux-Arts show in its presentation of beautiful objects (fig. 19). The exquisiteness of the eighty-seven drawings shown, however, was only part of the reason for this selective, noncomprehensive review of Le Corbusier's work: a more important purpose was to explore the process of architectural creativity, or "the visualizing process—the method of discourse—of an architect whose capacity for formal invention is unsurpassed."[29] Virtually all of the works were borrowed from the Fondation Le Corbusier, Paris, and were being exhibited publicly for the first time. As far as possible, preference in the selection of drawings was given to those that had remained in the architect's own hands. Unlike the *Le Corbusier: Architecture, Painting, Design* show in 1951, this exhibition made drawings its central focus.

By 1982, fifty years after the founding of the Department, 244 architectural drawings had joined the permanent collection.[30] The greater percentage of the over 700 architectural drawings in the collection today was still to come. Since the Department continued to acquire drawings out of its exhibitions, the exhibition program had a vital impact on the collection, particularly on its holdings of contemporary work. Also, as these acquisitions from the exhibition program entered the collection, they provided an inventory of architects, buildings, and themes to be supplemented and to inspire new purchases; the Department's ongoing fascination with visionary architecture, for example, which continues to this day, can be traced back to the *Visionary Architecture* exhibition of 1960. There has also been a persistent interest in building typologies, most notably the house, which has been used to promote modernist standards more than any other kind of structure.

19. *Le Corbusier: Architectural Drawings*, The Museum of Modern Art, New York, January 20–March 26, 1978. Installation view

Over the course of the Department's history, more than thirty exhibitions have explored the subject of the house or housing, most of them occurring during those first fifty years.[31] A few of these exhibitions featured full-scale constructions in The Abby Aldrich Rockefeller Sculpture Garden, beginning in 1941, with Fuller's Dymaxion Deployment Unit (fig. 20), and ending with the Japanese House in 1954–55, a structure of influential modernity and beauty (fig. 21).[32] The drawing collection includes numerous examples from these presentations, plus many others, ranging from Emil Hoppe's Villa Project of 1903 (p. 42) to Fuller's Dymaxion House Project of 1927–29 (pp. 64–65), from Mies's Farnsworth House of 1945–51 (p. 98) to Gaetano Pesce's Housing Unit for Two People Project of 1971 (p. 163). Not only does the house typology reveal the significant developments of architectural modernism, it is often the form that best characterizes a given architect's concerns and ideas.

In 1982 the Museum presented an exhibition entitled *The Architecture of Richard Neutra: From International Style to California Modern* (fig. 22). Focusing on Neutra's houses from the 1920s through the 1960s—"by far his most significant buildings," Drexler noted[33]—the show contained drawings and photographs in approximately equal balance, 110 and 134 respectively. Most of the drawings were borrowed from the Neutra Archive, part of the Department of Special Collections of the University Research Library at the University of California, Los Angeles. A significant number came from the years before Neutra emigrated to the United States, in 1923, and the Lovell House (1927–29), an acknowledged masterpiece of the modern movement, was also well represented. The drawings of the Miller House (c. 1953–56; p. 110) that are now in the collection were not included, although they had been on extended loan to the Department since 1980. They were finally acquired in 1985, a gift from the Miller family—and a fortunate one, since most of Neutra's drawings had by this time been given to the Neutra Archive.

20. *Buckminster Fuller's Dymaxion Deployment Unit*, The Museum of Modern Art, New York, October 10, 1941–April 1, 1942. Installation view

21. *Japanese Exhibition House*, The Museum of Modern Art, New York, June 16–October 21, 1954, and April 26–October 16, 1955. Installation view

22. *The Architecture of Richard Neutra: From International Style to California Modern*, The Museum of Modern Art, New York, July 21–October 12, 1982. Installation view showing photomural of Lovell House

An exhibition in 1985 looked at Ricardo Bofill and Leon Krier, two architects who had rejected the modernism that Neutra exemplified, and that had become so closely associated with the Museum (fig. 23). In fact Drexler brought them together precisely because they challenged what modern architecture had espoused and symbolized: Bofill has tried to reinstate a classical grandeur in his work, while Krier, who designs but does not build, "has virtually invented his own vernacular."[34] What Drexler did not discuss in his book was the beauty of the drawings, which gave the show a quality reminiscent of the earlier Beaux-Arts exhibition. Each architect has his own style (although some of the drawings of Bofill's projects, including the example here [p. 193], are produced by other renderers within his Taller de Arquitectura workshop), but the delicacy of Krier's drawings and the monumentality of Bofill's befit their respective subjects. These antimodernists provided not only an urban but an artistic conscience for the modern architect of the late 1980s.

Perhaps equally antithetical to early modernism is Deconstructivist architecture, with its fractured and discontinuous planes. Johnson, guest curator of a 1988 exhibition on the subject (fig. 24), defined the term:

Deconstructivist Architecture is not like the Russian Constructivism of the first quarter of the century. It certainly shares many of the forms—hence the name—but comes from a different source. . . . Deconstructivist Architecture stands for a fragmentation against totality, almost an amorphous and disconcerting mystique as against a rational clarity. It

23. *Ricardo Bofill and Leon Krier: Architecture, Urbanism, and History,* The Museum of Modern Art, New York, June 27–September 3, 1985. Installation view

has none of the baggage of utopian ideas and functionalist aims that the Russian movement had. . . . The characteristics of Deconstructivist Architecture, which are shared with the Russian pioneers, are in basic contrast to International Style modern. Wedges, lines, diagonals, warped planes take the place of orthogonal rectangles. Penetrations, fractures and parts take the place of wholes.[35]

The exhibition comprised ten projects, by Coop Himmelblau, Peter Eisenman, Frank Gehry, Zaha Hadid, Rem Koolhaas, Daniel Libeskind, and Bernard Tschumi. The drawings for two of these projects, Hadid's Peak Project (1983; p. 219) for Hong Kong and Tschumi's Parc de la Villette (1982–98; p. 217) for Paris, became part of the permanent collection in 1992. Although these drawings were not in the 1988 exhibition, they epitomize the principles it set forth.

Since the Wright exhibition of 1962, drawings have been integral, even favored parts of the Museum's architectural exhibitions. The Department has continued to produce shows that reflect its early aims: to present and collect good modern architecture from all over the world. Exhibitions such as *Emilio Ambasz/Steven Holl* (1989), *Roberto Burle Marx: The Unnatural Art of the Garden* (1991), and *Tadao Ando* (1991) featured drawings that both revealed significant works of architecture and were beautiful objects in themselves, and that, as such, ultimately joined the collection (fig. 25). Meanwhile developments in technology had enormously broadened the world of architectural drawing beyond the standard medium of graphite on paper. Computer-generated drawings, and various other forms of computerized display, assumed an appropriate place in exhibitions, just as they had been accorded an integral place in architects' offices. Although computer-aided design (CAD) had been used as early as the 1960s, it was not commonplace in architectural practice until relatively recently. The Department first acquired a computer-generated drawing in 1993; it also collected preliminary sketches for the same project, Arata Isozaki's Nara Convention Hall (1992–98; pp. 244–45). The purpose of these two types of drawing was different: the first

25. *Tadao Ando*, The Museum of Modern Art, New York, October 2–December 31, 1991. Installation view showing model and drawings of Chikatsu-Asuka Historical Museum

was a presentation drawing, the second described the development of the design. In that both of them preceded the building, they shared a chronology, but each had its own role.

Technology has also transformed exhibitions: far more than they could through the encompassing scale of the photomural, viewers can now enter a virtual world, and this one is interactive rather than passive. The 1999 exhibition *The Un-Private House*, organized by Riley, featured an interactive table that allowed visitors to take virtual tours of several of the buildings in the show. The 2001 exhibition *Mies in Berlin*, organized by Riley and guest curator Barry Bergdoll, contained digital models of a number of the architect's projects, both built and unbuilt, affording the viewer both interior and exterior perspectives and the ability to experience their relationship. Earlier exhibitions at the Museum had used drawings to help the viewer to determine a building's layout and program; the current computer-generated models can offer a more three-dimensional explanation.

In terms of future collecting, has the craft-intensive hand drawing finally won a respectable status in the art world only to be replaced by the computer-generated drawing? Will there be episodes of soul-searching over the status of drawing, of the kind that led to exhibitions such as *Frank Lloyd Wright Drawings*, in 1962, and *The Architecture of the Ecole des Beaux-Arts*, in 1975? Probably distinct types of drawing will coexist, as they always have. And as exhibitions increasingly provide outlets for architects to experiment with new forms of representation involving electronic technology, and these diverse mediums gain ground in daily architectural practice, the collection is likely to reflect their fullness and variety. No less than Lauretta Vinciarelli's evanescently beautiful watercolors (pp. 249–51), themselves a leap beyond the traditional architectural drawing, these works reveal that "architecture is body plus aura."[36] They and the other hundreds of drawings in the Museum's collection are testimony to the fact that drawing is very much alive in our contemporary world.

Notes

1. See John McAndrew and Janet Henrich, "Activities of the Department of Architecture since June 1939," memo to Alfred H. Barr, Jr., June 16, 1940, File 31.32b, box 31, Library Archives, The Museum of Modern Art.

2. "Report for the Department of Architecture, July 1, 1938–June 30, 1939," File 31.32b, box 31, Library Archives, The Museum of Modern Art.

3. Ibid.

4. On this exhibition see Terence Riley, *The International Style: Exhibition 15 and The Museum of Modern Art*, Columbia Books of Architecture, cat. 3 (New York: Rizzoli/CBA, 1992). The Department was called the Department of Architecture from 1932 to 1934 and the Department of Architecture and Industrial Art from 1935 to 1940. Between 1940 and 1948 the Department of Architecture and the Department of Industrial Design were two separate departments. Since 1948 the Department has been called the Department of Architecture and Design.

5. The seven models that entered the collection were Otto Haesler's Rothenburg Housing Development (later deaccessioned due to damage); Richard Neutra's Ring Plan School (later returned to the architect); Ludwig Mies van der Rohe's Tugendhat House; J. J. P. Oud's Project for a House at Pinehurst (later deaccessioned due to damage); Howe and Lescaze's Christie Forsythe Housing Project (later returned to the architects); Le Corbusier and Pierre Jeanneret's Villa Savoye; and Walter Gropius's Bauhaus School (later given to the Bauhaus).

6. An object was considered part of the collection when it was officially acquired and given an acquisition number. Although these Le Corbusier drawings were purchased in 1932, they were not taken into the collection and given acquisition numbers until 1947. The most likely explanation is that only models and photographs–the most accurate representations of the building or project–were collected at the time, and that since there was no model of the Swiss Pavilion, these drawings were acquired and used for study purposes.

7. The Museum's Staff Manual for 1952 contained the statement, "Buildings are included in the collection primarily for their merit as works of art, and with the popular acceptance of modern architecture in recent years, the reference file has become more selective than comprehensive." This statement referred to the extensive photographic files; nevertheless, it reveals the opinion that buildings were considered works of art. Staff Manual, 1952, "Museum Matters" 37.1, A&D, Library Archives, The Museum of Modern Art.

8. [Philip Johnson], "Need for a Department of Architecture," unpublished report dated 1932, Museum Archives, The Museum of Modern Art.

9. Eric Mendelsohn, quoted in Arnold Whittick, *Eric Mendelsohn* (London: Leonard Hill Limited, 1940), p. 181.

10. Mendelsohn, wall label, exhibition files for *Architecture of Eric Mendelsohn*, exhibition #159, November 26, 1941–January 4, 1942, Department of the Registrar, The Museum of Modern Art.

11. *Fortune* 18, no. 6 (December 1938): 75.

12. Ibid., p. 134.

13. On Mies's design for this exhibition see Riley, "Making History: Mies van der Rohe and The Museum of Modern Art," in Riley and Barry Bergdoll, *Mies in Berlin*, exh. cat. (New York: The Museum of Modern Art, 2001), pp. 11–23.

14. Photograph caption, exhibition files for *Mies van der Rohe*, September 16, 1947–January 25, 1948, exhibition #356, Department of the Registrar, The Museum of Modern Art.

15. "Work by Le Corbusier to be Shown at Museum," press release, exhibition files for *Le Corbusier: Architecture, Painting, Design*, July 3–August 12, 1951, Department of Architecture and Design, The Museum of Modern Art.

16. Roberto Burle Marx collaborated with Oscar Niemeyer on a number of projects, including the Beach House Project for Mr. and Mrs. Burton Tremaine, and in 1966 the Museum acquired a gouache by Burle Marx of the Tremaine garden plan.

17. Wall label, exhibition files for *From Le Corbusier to Niemeyer: 1929–1949*, February 15–April 3, 1949, Department of Architecture and Design, The Museum of Modern Art.

18. Frederick Kiesler, letter to Arthur Drexler, September 14, 1952, exhibition files for *Two Houses: New Ways to Build*, August 26–October 13, 1952, Department of Architecture and Design, The Museum of Modern Art.

19. The curatorial departments at the time were Architecture and Design, Drawings and Prints, Film, Painting and Sculpture, and Photography. Since then the structure has been reorganized: the curatorial departments today are Architecture and Design, Drawings, Film and Media, Painting and Sculpture, Photography, and Prints and Illustrated Books.

20. Drawings by many of the participants in the exhibition–Hans Poelzig, Kiesler, Le Corbusier, Michael Webb, Paul Nelson, Paolo Soleri, and Louis Kahn–were acquired at various points years later.

21. Drexler, *Visionary Architecture*, exh. brochure (New York: The Museum of Modern Art, 1960), n.p. This passage also appeared as a wall label.

22. Drexler, letter to William Wesley Peters, January 26, 1961, exhibition files for *Frank Lloyd Wright Drawings*, March 14–May 6, 1962, Department of Architecture and Design, The Museum of Modern Art.

23. Drexler, *The Drawings of Frank Lloyd Wright*, exh. cat. (New York: Horizon Press for The Museum of Modern Art, 1962), p. 7.

24. Mildred Schmertz, "Frank Lloyd Wright, Draftsman," *Architectural Record* 131 (June 1962): 48.

25. Drexler, wall text, exhibition files for *Ludwig Mies van der Rohe: Drawings in the Collection of The Museum of Modern Art*, February 2–March 23, 1966, Department of Architecture and Design, The Museum of Modern Art.

26. This exhibition had originally been titled *Contemporary Viennese Architecture*.

27. Drexler, "Engineer's Architecture: Truth and Its Consequences," in Drexler, ed., *The Architecture of the Ecole des Beaux-Arts*, exh cat., with essays by Richard Chafee, Drexler, Neil Levine, and David Van Zanten (New York: The Museum of Modern Art, 1977), p. 24.

28. Drexler, "The Architecture of the Ecole des Beaux-Arts," ms., exhibition files for *The Architecture of the Ecole des Beaux-Arts*, October 29, 1975–January 4, 1976, Department of Architecture and Design, The Museum of Modern Art.

29. Press release, exhibition files for *Le Corbusier: Architectural Drawings*, January 20–March 26, 1978, Department of Architecture and Design, The Museum of Modern Art.

30. This figure excludes all of the Mies drawings that became part of the Mies van der Rohe Archive in 1968.

31. According to an unofficial departmental chronology, the Department organized thirty-one exhibitions on houses or housing between 1932 and 1982, and three between 1983 and 2001. This does not include exhibitions that included a combination of houses and other building types.

32. Exhibition houses by Marcel Breuer and Gregory Ain were also shown in the Garden, in 1949 and 1950 respectively. Three structures by Buckminster Fuller were installed there in 1959, but none of these was a "house." For more information regarding exhibition houses at the Museum see Peter Reed, "The MoMA Exhibition House," in *Visions of the Real: Modern Houses in the 20th Century*, vol. 2 of a special issue of *A+U* (2000).

33. Drexler, Preface, in Drexler and Thomas S. Hines, *The Architecture of Richard Neutra: From International Style to California Modern*, exh. cat. (New York: The Museum of Modern Art, 1982), n.p. [3].

34. Drexler, *Ricardo Bofill and Leon Krier: Architecture, Urbanism, and History*, exh. cat. (New York: The Museum of Modern Art, 1985), p.12.

35. Johnson, "Deconstructivist Architecture–June 1988, Description," ms., exhibition files for *Deconstructivist Architecture*, June 23–August 30, 1988, Department of Architecture and Design, The Museum of Modern Art.

36. Joan Ockman, "Dialogue in Second Person Singular for Lauretta," in Brooke Hodge, ed., *Not Architecture but Evidence That It Exists: Lauretta Vinciarelli, Watercolors*, exh. cat. (Cambridge, Mass.: Harvard University Graduate School of Design, and New York: Princeton Architectural Press, 1998), n.p. The purchase of Vinciarelli's *Variations and Interferences of 3 Non-Homogenous Grids in a 32 x 32 cm Square*, in 1974, was the Department's first acquisition of architectural drawings by a woman.

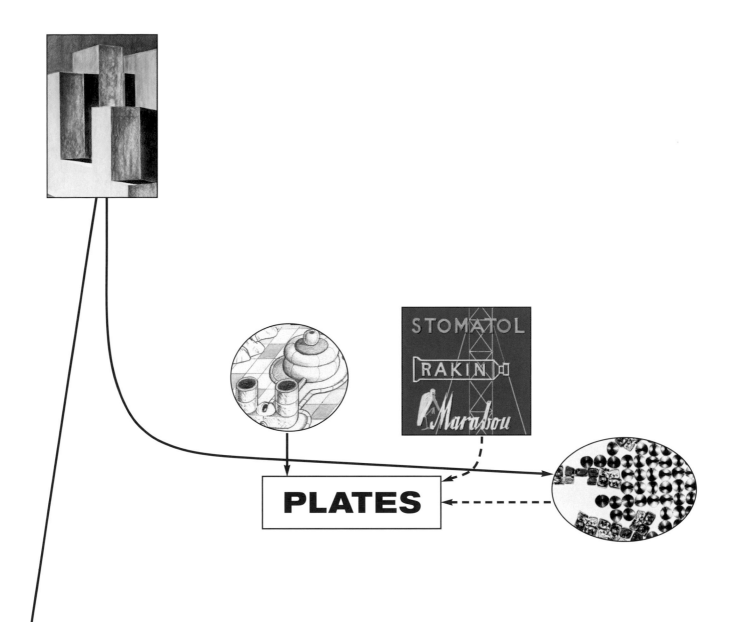

PLATES

A Note on the Plates

The word "project" in the titles of the works illustrated here indicates that the design exists only on paper—that it was never built. The captions include the dates both for the entire project to which each drawing relates and for the drawing itself; where those dates are the same, a single date appears alone. In the dimensions, height precedes width. Where a renderer other than the architect has been identified for any drawing, the caption supplies his or her name. All drawings are in the collection of The Museum of Modern Art.

Otto Wagner

Ferdinandsbrücke Project, Vienna, Austria

Elevation, preliminary version. Project: 1896–1905. Drawing: 1896. Ink on paper with collaged text, 19⅛ × 66½" (48.6 × 168.9 cm)

In 1857, four years before Otto Wagner completed his architectural studies, the Austro-Hungarian Emperor Franz Josef agreed to demands that the medieval fortifications of Vienna be demolished, as they were in so many European cities during the nineteenth century. The opening of the Old City—the *Aldtstadt*—to modern expansion provided stunning opportunities to a generation of architects among whom Wagner would emerge as the leading figure.

In 1895 Wagner declared, "The only possible point of departure for our artistic creation is modern life." His design for the Ferdinandsbrücke, a bridge to be named in honor of Archduke Francis Ferdinand, is a frank expression of the techniques of modern engineering. The bridge's exposed steel truss was to span the Danube Canal in a low broad arch. Adorning the structure are imperial emblems—coats of arms, wreaths, and garlands—appropriate to Vienna as the capital of the Austro-Hungarian Empire. Over a century later the decorative aspects of Wagner's design might seem dominant. To the contemporaneous viewer, however, accustomed to the sumptuous Baroque buildings of imperial Vienna, the bridge would have looked startlingly modern. Reaching for metaphors, critics and admirers alike noted the "nakedness" and "masculinity" of Wagner's designs for monumental civic works.

The large scale of the drawing is complemented by the delicacy of the ink rendering and the stylized lettering. The work's aesthetic qualities reflect Wagner's position as an architect teaching within a fine arts institution; they affirm the idea that art, architecture, and design all contribute to the creation of a *Gesamtkunstwerk*—an environment aspiring to be a "total work of art." Wagner's commitment to this ideal, as well as his spectacular skills in producing beautiful drawings, are evident in the work of his students, most notably Emil Hoppe and Marcel Kammerer, both of whom would later work in Wagner's office.

Wagner's prolific output and progressive ideas influenced an entire generation and firmly established him as a forefather of modern architecture. He argued for simplicity and a new, "realist" style that implied designers should use modern materials and clear methods of construction. The Ferdinandsbrücke was not built to his design, but as Vienna expanded outside its medieval boundaries, he did complete many projects in the city according to these principles, including the 1898 network of stations for the newly built U-Bahn light rail system, the Steinhof Church (1902), and the Postal Savings Bank (1903).

—Terence Riley

Marcel Kammerer
Royal Hunting Tent Project

Exterior perspective (below). 1900. Ink, graphite, watercolor, gouache, and airbrush on paper, 18⅞ × 12⅜" (47.9 × 31.4 cm). Gift of Jo Carole and Ronald S. Lauder, 1997

Emil Hoppe
Villa Project, outside Vienna, Austria

Exterior perspective (right). 1903. Graphite, color pencil, ink, and gouache on tracing paper, 15⅛ × 7½" (38.4 × 19.1 cm). Gift of Jo Carole and Ronald S. Lauder, 1997

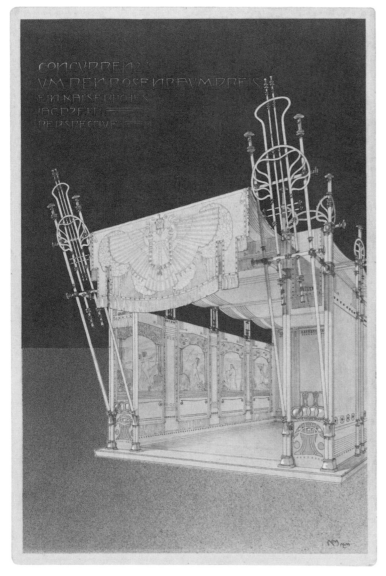

Frank Lloyd Wright
Unity Temple, Oak Park, Illinois

Exterior perspective and partial plan. Project: 1905–8. Drawing:
c. 1929–30. Ink and graphite on paper, 23¼ × 34⅞" (59 × 88.5 cm).
Drawing attributed to Heinrich Klumb and Takehiko Okami. Patricia Phelps
de Cisneros Purchase Fund, The Lauder Foundation (Leonard and Evelyn
Lauder Fund), and Victoria Newhouse Purchase Fund, 1999

Although this drawing of Frank Lloyd Wright's Unity Temple is inscribed with the building's completion date, 1908, the rendering itself was made years later, around 1929–30. This fact is significant because the drawing's style and the circumstances of its production relate directly to the aging architect's reputation and waning career, which, in 1930, when Wright was in his early sixties, were being challenged by a younger generation associated with the emerging modern movement that would come to be known as the International Style. That year, delivering the Kahn Lectures on Modern Architecture at Princeton University, Wright critiqued aspects of the new architecture. A small exhibition of his work that accompanied the lectures featured many of his projects from the century's first decade—including Unity Temple, an influential building that boldly broke with traditions of ecclesiastical architecture in form, materials, and symbolism. In an effort to recast Wright's work in a more modern guise, his young assistants Heinrich Klumb and Takehiko Okami prepared new drawings for the show in a bold new manner.

In this rendering Unity Temple is reduced to starkly contrasting, relatively unornamented black and white planes, and is completely detached from its context in the landscape. The drawing focuses our attention on the cubic massing of the monolithic reinforced-concrete building, the vertical and horizontal planar surfaces, and the corner piers containing the stairs, evident in the plan below. The style is a marked departure from Wright's more typical renderings, which are romantic and colorful, expressively depicting the building, its details, and the surrounding landscape. By effectively co-opting the drawing style of a younger generation of architects associated with the modern movement, Wright consciously positioned himself as a forerunner of the so-called International Style.

—Peter Reed

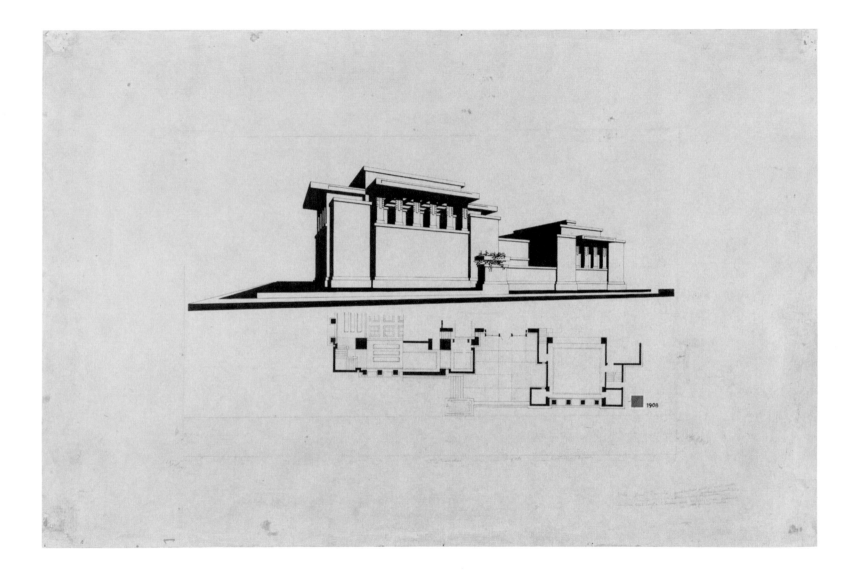

Frank Lloyd Wright

American System-Built Houses for the Richards Company. Model D101

Exterior perspective. Project: 1915–17. Drawing: c. 1915–17. Lithograph, 11 × 8½" (27.9 × 21.6 cm). Drawing attributed to Antonin Raymond. David Rockefeller, Jr., Fund, Ira Howard Levy Fund, and Jeffrey P. Klein Purchase Fund, 1993

American System-Built Houses for the Richards Company. Unspecified model

Plan oblique. Project: 1915–17. Drawing: c. 1915–17. Lithograph, 11 × 8½" (27.9 × 21.6 cm). Drawing attributed to Antonin Raymond. David Rockefeller, Jr., Fund, Ira Howard Levy Fund, and Jeffrey P. Klein Purchase Fund, 1993

"**Y**ou Can Own an American Home," trumpeted a 1917 Chicago newspaper's full-page advertisement for Frank Lloyd Wright's new "System-Built Houses"—low-cost houses assembled from factory-produced elements. Customers requesting plans and brochures from the Richards Company would have received prints like these illustrating the many house models from which they could have chosen. Modeled on Japanese woodblock prints, the style of Wright's lithographs evinces his life-long love of Japanese art. The high horizon line, the planar flatness of foreground and sky, the silhouetted foliage, and the red square (or "chop") framed by the text—all suggest a studied *japonisme*. Most likely the originals were prepared by Antonin Raymond, Wright's assistant on the contemporary Imperial Hotel project in Tokyo.

The System-Built Houses were Wright's first experiment with mass production. Like many modern architects, he confronted both the benefits of the rationalized standardization associated with machine production and the desire for individual expression. "Individuality is a national ideal," Wright proclaimed in 1910, and for him this ideal was symbolized by the American house. Thus he developed a system that allowed variety within an overall unity. Regardless of house size and plan, most of the details were "conventionalized," a term Wright applied to a principle of abstracting form to its essentials. The houses were constructed of wood framing, floors, joists, rafters, roofs, and trim. To streamline the construction process, lumber was measured and precut in the Richards Company factory, then shipped to the site where it was to be assembled, thus saving the contractor and the customer time and money.

Wright liked to give his houses descriptive names, for example La Miniatura (pp. 62–63), but the System-Built Houses bear perfunctory labels, such as D101. There were dozens of models, ranging from one to three stories, and the isometric plans illustrate numerous room configurations as well as ideas on how to furnish them. The designs recall Wright's earlier Prairie Houses, named for the landscape of his native Midwest. The characteristic low cantilevered roofs, the linear wood trim visually unifying the stucco wall planes, and the geometric decoration of the art-glass windows constitute a compelling modern alternative to the typical suburban bungalow. An untold number of System-Built Houses were built, mostly in the Midwest. In the following decades Wright continued to experiment with a range of materials and construction systems in an effort to reduce the expense of house building and to give industrialized methods character, expression, and personality.

—Peter Reed

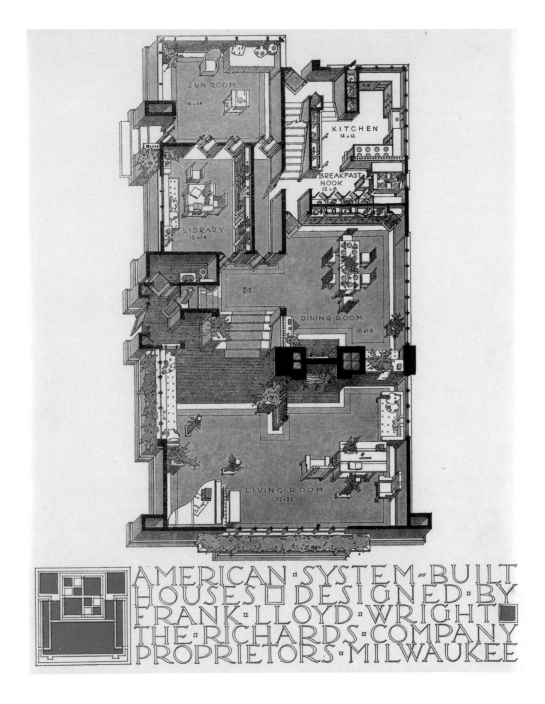

Erik Gunnar Asplund

Woodland Chapel, Woodland Cemetery, Stockholm, Sweden

Side elevation. Project: chapel, 1918–21; cemetery, 1915–40. Drawing: c. 1918–20. Graphite and crayon on tracing paper, 8¼ × 10½" (21 × 26.7 cm) (irreg.). Marshall Cogan Purchase Fund, 1984

Woodland Crematorium, Woodland Cemetery, Stockholm, Sweden

Site plan and section, final version. Project: crematorium, 1935–40; cemetery, 1915–40. Drawing: 1937. Graphite on tracing paper, 16¼ × 37⅞" (41.3 × 96.2 cm). Gift of Mrs. John D. Rockefeller 3rd, Mrs. Gifford Phillips, Celeste and Armand P. Bartos, and Mrs. S. I. Newhouse, Jr., and purchase, 1990

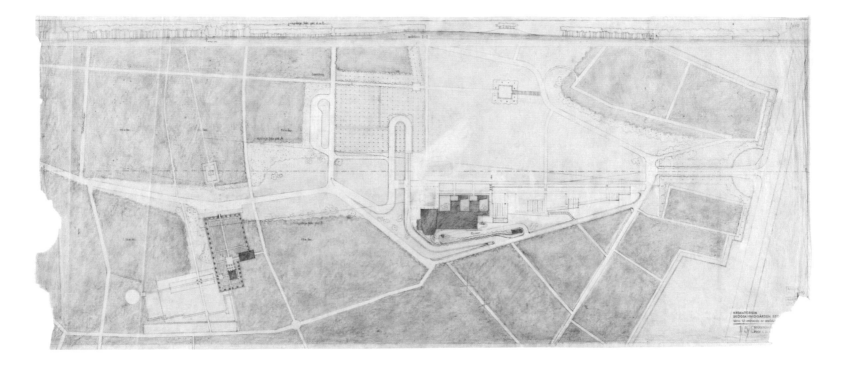

In 1915, Erik Gunnar Asplund and Sigurd Lewerentz, now recognized as two of Sweden's leading twentieth-century architects, won a competition to expand the South Stockholm Cemetery. The commission would span their entire careers, reflecting stylistic developments and shifts over a twenty-five-year period.

Asplund's early sketch of the Woodland Chapel, which he was directly commissioned to design, reflects the influence of Swedish Romanticism. His proposal—"a synthesis of temple and hut," according to the architectural historian Caroline Constant—was directly inspired by a vernacular cottage in Liselund, Denmark, that he visited on his honeymoon in 1918. The chapel is set in a pine forest. A path leads through the wood to the entrance, where the dominant form is a steeply pitched shingle roof, a massive shape like a truncated pyramid supported by columns. The deep portico continues the darkness of the forest. Only when the doors to the chapel are open is the visitor presented with a light-filled interior.

This preliminary sketch has a childlike quality, but nevertheless captures the essence of the building's strong geometric forms. It also reflects Asplund's initial interest in making the form of the chapel follow the terrain, so that where the land dips it exposes a visible and directly accessible basement level. He later changed this design in order to reinforce the cubic volume of the chapel itself.

The site plan for the cemetery evolved dramatically over the course of the project, reaching its definitive form, an open spatial arrangement, by 1932. In a drawing by Asplund from 1937, showing the northern part of the site, the entrance to the cemetery is represented by a semicircle on the right side of the drawing. From here, a walled allée marks a strong axial movement to the south, interrupted when it opens to present the visitor with a tranquil rolling landscape devoid of graves. Asplund and Lewerentz studied this entry sequence carefully, establishing it as both monumental and contemplative to communicate the importance of nature, to which all living things ultimately return. As Asplund had in devising the walled and forested precinct around the Woodland Chapel (the rectangular form on the left side of the drawing), which is discreetly surrounded by the crematorium and other ancillary buildings, they saved monumentality for the landscape, rather than trying to achieve it through any structure or object. By the time of Asplund's death, in 1940, the architects had transformed their forested site into a modern sanctuary for death and bereavement.

—Matilda McQuaid

Hans Poelzig
Concert Hall Project, Dresden, Germany

Interior perspective, preliminary version. 1918. Color pencil and graphite on tracing paper, 14⅝ × 16⅛" (37.1 × 41 cm). Gift of Henry G. Proskauer, 1966

Hans Poelzig made this drawing for a concert hall while he was the city architect of Dresden, a position he held from 1916 to 1920. A painter and set designer as well as an architect, he was then at the beginning of the Expressionist phase for which he is best known. Stressing the subjective over the objective, Expressionist architects such as Poelzig, Bruno Taut, and Hans Scharoun searched for personal and emotional architectural forms, and their designs had a dynamic quality that reflected or commented upon the building's intended function and revealed inner meaning through structure.

The forms of Expressionist architecture tended to be symbolic and visionary—often literally so, in that, because of World War I, and Germany's depressed economic situation in the years that followed it, Poelzig and his peers produced more paper architecture than built work. Yet Poelzig,

although he relentlessly sketched anything that caught his eye, felt that sketching "as an end to itself began the ruination of architecture." The drawing for its own sake that occurred in the academies, he believed, ran to excess, and resulted in a loss of architectonic culture and, for architects, a loss of feeling for three-dimensional space. Even so, and however Poelzig's Concert Hall might have been realized, this detail has its own stature. Natural, organic, plantlike forms create a fanciful and romantic setting, and almost baroque ornamental patterns radiate from the stage, their rhythm evoking the music they were designed to house.

—Bevin Cline

Ludwig Mies van der Rohe
Friedrichstrasse Skyscraper Project, Berlin-Mitte, Germany

Exterior perspective from north. 1921. Charcoal and graphite on paper mounted on board, 68¼ × 48" (173.4 × 121.9 cm). Mies van der Rohe Archive, gift of the architect, 1966

This design for a crystal tower, conceived by the German architect Ludwig Mies van der Rohe, was unprecedented in 1921. It was based on the untried idea that a supporting steel skeleton would be able to free the exterior walls from their load-bearing function, allowing a building to have a surface more translucent than solid. A number of American skyscrapers had featured expanses of glass, but Mies was the first to imagine such a building without a structural or decorative frame of masonry. Indeed Mies seems to have been inspired by photographs of American skyscrapers when they were still under construction, a stage that he felt revealed "the bold constructive thoughts, and then the impression of the high-reaching steel skeletons is overpowering."

Mies developed his radical proposal in response to a call for German architects to design Berlin's first skyscraper, intended for a triangular site bounded by the Spree River, the busy shopping street Friedrichstrasse, and the train station of the same name. The competition drew 140 entries as well as intense interest from architects, artists, and the general public, generating debate about the future of the city and representing hopes for new beginnings after Germany's defeat in World War I. While Mies's bold image of an entirely steel-and-glass skyscraper had a solid scientific and technological basis, his crystal-shaped plan reflected the more fantastic visions of Expressionist architects and artists, who were drawn to glass as a symbol of purity and renewal.

This very large drawing was repeatedly reproduced in publications around the world, achieving iconic status. In 1964, the architect, who had left it behind when he emigrated to the United States in 1938, was able to retrieve it from what was then East Germany, and it has been exhibited frequently at The Museum of Modern Art since then. Its bold image and masterful draftsmanship continue to inspire.

—Terence Riley

Hugh Ferriss
Buildings in the Modeling Project

Aerial perspective. 1924. Conté crayon on board, 12½ × 32"
(54.6 × 81.3 cm). Gift of Mrs. Hugh Ferriss, 1966

Hugh Ferriss was the most prominent urban portraitist in the American architecture world of the 1920s and '30s. Working as a delineator for architects such as Cass Gilbert and Raymond Hood, he rendered the evolution of both the real and the ideal metropolis.

Ferriss claimed that his role as an architectural delineator was "to tell the truth about a building," which meant capturing not only its form and mass but also its mood and personality. His favorite subject was the skyscraper. When the New York Zoning Law of 1916 limited the bulk of skyscrapers by requiring setbacks and height restrictions, Ferriss rendered the extraordinary effects of these regulations on architectural form, working sometimes on commissions dealing with actual buildings, sometimes on more visionary studies for the metropolis. Both of these kinds of drawing, including *Buildings in the Modeling*, were compiled in his 1929 book *The Metropolis of Tomorrow.*

Specifically, *Buildings in the Modeling* offered an image of how buildings could be shaped or "modeled" in order to retain the maximum mass while remaining within the Zoning Law. The chiseled towers, drawn with a Conté crayon to create a soft, chiaroscuro effect, appear simultaneously dense and transparent; they also suggest a dramatic vision of the city center. Rejecting the deurbanized American landscape advocated by Frank Lloyd Wright, Ferriss promoted the idea of a concentrated metropolis, a major center of commerce, art, science, and technology. Although the buildings in his vision of the metropolis are simple, unadorned masses, each dramatically captures the psychological impact of the soaring skyscraper on twentieth-century Americans.

—Matilda McQuaid

Frank Lloyd Wright

St. Mark's-in-the-Bouwerie Towers Project, New York City, New York

Aerial perspective. Project: 1927–31. Drawing: c. 1927–31. Graphite and color pencil on tracing paper, 23¾ × 15" (60.3 × 38 cm). Jeffrey P. Klein Purchase Fund, Barbara Pine Purchase Fund, and Frederieke Taylor Purchase Fund, 1999

FIRST GROUP

IN THE BOUWERIE. NEW YORK CITY FRANK LLOYD WRIGHT. ARCHITECT

Theo van Doesburg (Christian Emil Marie Küpper) and Cornelis van Eesteren

Contra-Construction Project

Axonometric. 1923. Gouache on lithograph on paper, 22½ × 22½" (57.2 × 57.2 cm). Gift of Edgar Kaufmann, Jr., 1947

With the zeal of a crusader, Theo van Doesburg, the prolific writer, painter, and cofounder of the avant-garde Dutch movement de Stijl, promoted a new order uniting art and life. In his utopian quest for a universal ideal, cleansed of social and artistic conventions but not without moral and spiritual dimensions, van Doesburg predicated a formal language of abstraction on the rectangle, primary colors (red, blue, and yellow), and asymmetrically balanced compositions. To suggest what a de Stijl environment might look like, van Doesburg enlisted the assistance of the architect Cornelis van Eesteren. In 1923 the two men mounted a landmark exhibition at Léonce Rosenberg's Galerie L'Effort Moderne in Paris. This so-called "Contra-Construction" was among the works exhibited.

The Contra-Construction is not a study for a specific building but a meditation on a new kind of architectural space and structure. Serving as a demonstration of the ideas in the artists' manifestos, the composition—an axonometric placed diagonally on the paper—is key to understanding their aims. The construction seems to float on the sheet, divorced from time or place. The high vantage point lets us see many sides at once, but we have no clear understanding of front, side, or back, or of inside and out. Horizontal and vertical planes define a complex of asymmetrical volumes around a central open core. Color is a constructive element, applied to elements running the height, length, and width of the construction. The planes have an atectonic character, being divorced from a supporting function. The spatial relations and sense of freedom in the composition underscore van Doesburg's overarching goal: to liberate humanity from material things through a new form of modernism.

—Peter Reed

Albrecht Heubner
Minimal Dwelling Project

c. 1928. Cut-and-pasted printed papers, gouache, and graphite on paper,
11¾ × 14¾" (29.9 × 37.4 cm). Acquired through Walter Gropius, 1977

die mindestwohnung

Ludwig Mies van der Rohe
Concrete Country House Project, no intended site known

Exterior perspective, garden facade. 1923. Pastel and graphite on paper, 33¾ × 90" (85.8 × 228.5 cm). Mies van der Rohe Archive, gift of the architect, 1968

Frank Lloyd Wright
La Miniatura, Mrs. George Madison Millard House, Pasadena, California

Exterior perspective. 1923. Color pencil and graphite on paper, 20¾ × 19⅝" (52.2 × 50 cm). Gift of Mr. and Mrs. Walter Hochschild, 1981

The romance that Frank Lloyd Wright found in the landscape and climate of Southern California is captured in his seductive rendering of "La Miniatura"—the name he gave to the small house he designed for Mrs. George Madison Millard. The perspective from the garden depicts the house in its lush surroundings, enshrouded by trees and overlooking a small pond. Wright recounted his discovery of the site in his autobiography: "My eyes had fallen upon a ravishing ravine . . . in which stood two beautiful eucalyptus trees. . . . No one would want to build down in a ravine out there." Color pencil was Wright's favorite drawing medium, and it was well suited for this impressionistic picture.

La Miniatura was the first in a series known as the Textile Block houses that Wright designed in the 1920s. It is constructed out of a combination of plain-faced and ornamental concrete blocks, which were cast on site from molds designed by Wright. These square blocks, some of them perforated with glass-filled apertures, form a continuous interior and exterior fabric, and their relatively small scale allows for a design that closely follows the contours of the landscape. The rendering shows how the house relates to the site, and how the intricate decoration of the textured blocks echoes the dappled light of the dense foliage.

In his Textile Block houses Wright attempted to develop a flexible building system, marrying the merits of standardized machine production to his own innovative creative vision. As such, La Miniatura brilliantly reflects his intention to create what he described as "a distinctly genuine expression of California in terms of modern industry and American life."

—Peter Reed

RESIDENCE FOR MRS. GEORGE MADISON MILLARD ... FRANK LLOYD WRIGHT ... ARCHITECT

R. Buckminster Fuller

Dymaxion House Project

Plan. Project: 1927–29. Drawing: c. 1927. Graphite, watercolor, and metallic ink on tracing paper, 10¾ × 10" (27.3 × 25.4 cm) (irreg.). Gift of The Howard Gilman Foundation, 2000

Dymaxion House Project

Elevation, axonometric, and plan. Project: 1927–29. Drawing: 1927. Graphite and watercolor on paper, 32⅞ × 19" (83.5 × 48.3 cm). Gift of The Howard Gilman Foundation, 2000

"**H**ow much does your house weigh?" This typical provocation by Buckminster Fuller was aimed at critics of his Dymaxion House, a radically new environment for dwelling introduced in 1927 and so named for its "maximum gain of advantage from minimal energy input." This 1,600-square-foot house weighed only three tons; its cost was about the same as the price of a car. The dream of a low-cost factory-built house captured the attention of many socially conscious architects in the twentieth century: if the automobile industry could mass-produce their products quickly, efficiently, and relatively cheaply, why couldn't a similar system be applied to housing? Perhaps no one pushed this idea as

far as Fuller, an extraordinary genius, inventor, philosopher, architect, and engineer.

In the Dymaxion House, a central aluminum mast contains all the mechanical elements of the building in its core. Two hexagonal decks are suspended from this mast by triangulated tension cables. The house is enclosed within walls of double-panel vacuum glazing and is a fully air-conditioned environment. One of Fuller's students called the Dymaxion House a "metallurgical pound cake," and indeed the rooms are divided into wedge shapes, seen most clearly in the color-coded plan.

The unconventional shape, structure, and materials of the Dymaxion House stood in sharp contrast to buildings by leading modernists such as Le Corbusier and Mies van der Rohe. Le Corbusier had described his own mass-produced housing as a "machine for living in," and the Dymaxion House was unabashedly machinelike, but Fuller was highly critical of modern European architects, who he felt were preoccupied with cosmetic concerns that merely symbolized or aestheticized functional elements without a clear and honest display of function and efficiency.

The Dymaxion House never went into production, but after World War II, Fuller introduced a new version, the aluminum Wichita House, to be manufactured by the aircraft industry. Although several thousand advance orders were received, only one was built; the enterprise collapsed under bureaucratic delays. Fuller went on to design the famous Geodesic Dome, which applied some of the same principles of efficiency, shape, system, and materials that he had explored in the Dymaxion House. His work inspired many architects, but he was also accused of being overly technical at the expense of aesthetic merit, a charge to which he responded, "I never work with aesthetic considerations in mind, but I have a test: if something isn't beautiful when I get finished with it, it's no good."

—Peter Reed

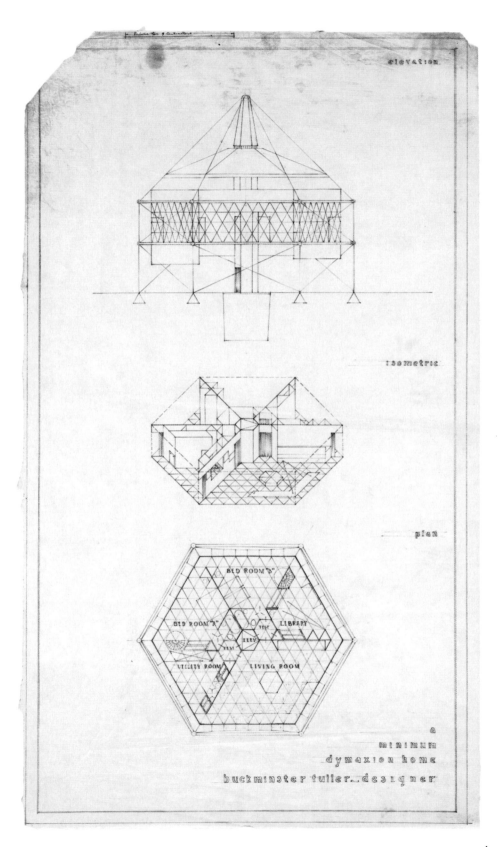

Theo van Doesburg (Christian Emil Marie Küpper)

Café Aubette, Strasbourg, France

Color scheme for floor and long walls of ballroom, preliminary version. Project: 1926–28. Drawing: 1927. Ink and gouache on paper, 21 × 14¾" (53.3 × 37.5 cm). Gift of Lily Auchincloss, Celeste Bartos, and Marshall Cogan, 1982

Plan d. Parquet avec 2 mins.

Leonard aux bourg arch.
Paris

Le Corbusier (Charles-Édouard Jeanneret)
Urban Studies Projects for Montevideo, Uruguay, and São Paulo, Brazil

Aerial perspectives; Montevideo, above; São Paulo, below. 1929. Ink on paper, 10⅝ × 6½" (27 × 16.5 cm). Emilio Ambasz Fund, 1985

At the end of the 1920s, Le Corbusier's grand plan for the future of the city was evolving rapidly: the layered and open-ended scheme of his *Ville contemporaine* of 1922 was developing into the linearity and political homogeneity of his *Ville radieuse* of 1930–31, which these sketches anticipate. Le Corbusier visited South America in 1929, a memorable trip that allowed him to survey the tropical landscapes and cityscapes from the air at leisure, with the help of the aviators Jean Mermoz and Antoine de Saint-Exupéry. The uniqueness of the landscape, and the contrast between the forest and open terrain and the sprawling, suffocating cities, inspired him to draw up new plans for Montevideo and São Paulo.

The sketch for Montevideo, at the top of the drawing, highlights a giant business center under a motorway that juts into the bay, connecting the most important buildings and bypassing the preexisting urban chaos. The plan for São Paulo, below, attempts to dodge the city's traffic by setting a cruciform arrangement of motorways on the roofs of residential apartment blocks. Making powerful strokes and cuts through the landscape, Le Corbusier envisions superimposing buildings and freeways on a giant scale over the existing urban fabric. Instead of a center, the new city would have satellites and zones, all with their own infrastructural systems.

"I prefer drawing to talking. Drawing is faster, and allows less room for lies," Le Corbusier remarked in 1961. These sketches testify to the strength of his ideas' flow onto the paper.

—Paola Antonelli

Ludwig Mies van der Rohe

German Pavilion, Barcelona, Spain

Interior perspective. Project: 1928–29. Drawing: c. 1928–29. Graphite on illustration board, 39 × 51¼" (99.1 × 130.2 cm). Mies van der Rohe Archive, gift of the architect, 1968

Late in 1928, Mies van der Rohe began to design the pavilion that would represent Germany at the 1929 Barcelona International Exposition, the first such event in which the country had participated since its defeat in World War I. The democratically elected postwar government had made its aspirations for the pavilion clear: the building was to represent "our desire to be absolutely truthful, giving voice to the spirit of a new era." The state made few other demands, leaving Mies free to pursue his most radical architectural expression of free-flowing space, bounded only by rich but abstract surfaces of Tinian marble, mirror chrome, plate glass, and onyx.

Since the pavilion was demolished when the fair was over, relatively few later audiences and architectural critics had ever seen the building except through the filter of period black-and-white photographs, and its significance became largely a matter of thirdhand debate rather than actual experience. In time it came to be interpreted in terms of Mies's later, more rational work of the 1940s and after, often derided as simple "glass boxes." This unfinished and little-published rendering of the interior, however, reveals another attitude, more sensual than objective. To the right of the column whose outlines are sketched in the center of the drawing, Mies carefully renders the view from the main space through a glass wall into the courtyard, with its reflecting pool and a sculpture of a reclining figure. Rather than making the glass look fully transparent, he gives the dark green Tinian marble different shadings behind the wall and to the left and right of it, approximating the visual effect of the screen of gray glass. Even the reflection of the sculpture in the pool is studiously considered.

—Terence Riley

Erik Gunnar Asplund

Stockholm Exhibition, Stockholm, Sweden

Elevation of advertising tower. Project: 1928–30. Drawing: 1930. Gouache on board, 20¾ × 13" (52.7 × 33 cm). Gift of Frederieke Taylor and purchase, 1990

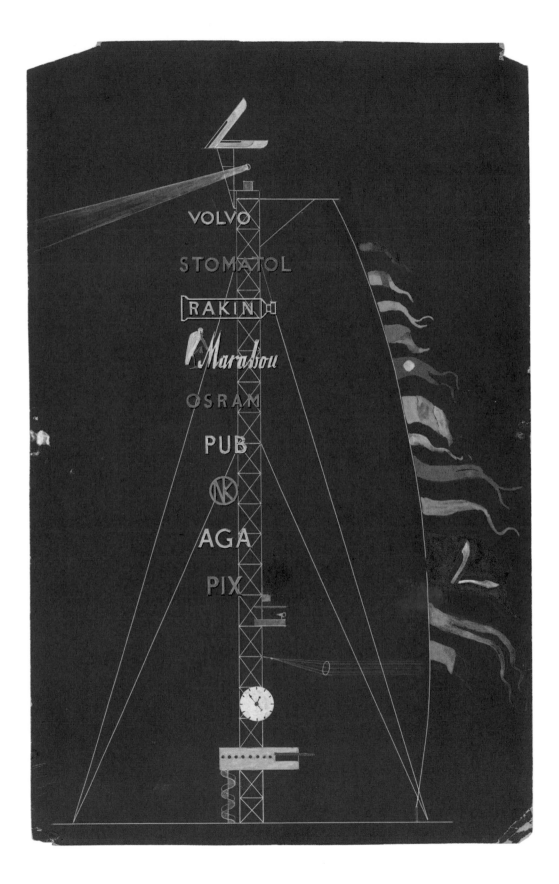

Le Corbusier (Charles-Édouard Jeanneret) and Pierre Jeanneret
Swiss Pavilion, Cité internationale universitaire de Paris, France

Perspective of north and west elevations. Project: 1930–32. Drawing: 1932. Lithograph and airbrush on paper, 26⅛ × 44¼" (66.4 × 112.4 cm). Purchase, 1947

This serene lateral perspective of Le Corbusier's and Pierre Jeanneret's Swiss Pavilion conceals the difficulty of the conditions in which the building was realized. The Cité internationale universitaire de Paris had been founded in 1921 to accommodate foreign students in the city. Architecturally it had grown rapidly into a collection of often sappy, overstyled buildings, each associated with one of the nations represented at the university. Le Corbusier and his cousin and associate Pierre Jeanneret at first refused the commission for the Swiss Pavilion, which was offered to them in 1930 by the Comité des universités suisses. The president of the Cité universitaire himself felt that the allotted budget was inadequate; in addition, the building was to sit on soft, unsteady soil that would make the foundations hard to calculate and build. Yet Le Corbusier and Jeanneret finally accepted the commission.

Charles-Édouard Jeanneret—Le Corbusier—was among the most innovative and revolutionary architects of the twentieth century. Even before adopting his famous pseudonym, in 1920, he had set out to revise the creative relationships between engineering and architecture and between architecture and art. His and Pierre Jeanneret's manifesto essay *5 Points d'une architecture nouvelle* (1926), only one among his many opinionated contributions to the field, laid out five features he considered basic to the new architecture, and all of these features but one, the roof garden, appear in the scheme for the Swiss Pavilion: the *pilotis* elevating the building off the ground; the free plan, in which the weight of the building is borne by columns separated from the building's outer walls, allowing a flexible interior space; the free facade, a consequence of the free plan; and the long horizontal windows.

Not only is the finished Swiss Pavilion beautiful in its efficiency, it also anticipated a new way of building entire city neighborhoods. This presentation drawing shows a building that could indeed be a proud element of Le Corbusier's *Ville radieuse*, the model of the ideal city that the architect was developing and that he would first publicize in 1933. Le Corbusier's signature *pilotis*, transformed here into sturdier pylons, provide an intuitive and fluid solution to pedestrian circulation. The orientation of the building to absorb as much healthy sunlight as possible, and the disposition of the public and private spaces, testify to Le Corbusier's idealistic belief in the power of architecture to organize and uplift individuals and whole communities.

—Paola Antonelli

Lilly Reich

The Dwelling of Our Time, German Building Exhibition, Berlin, Germany

Plan and elevation of interior-finishing-materials exhibit, gallery of Hall II. 1931. Graphite on tracing paper, 21¾ × 30⅜" (55.2 × 77.1 cm). Mies van der Rohe Archive, gift of the architect, 1968

The Dwelling of Our Time, German Building Exhibition, Berlin, Germany

Elevation, section, and plan of turnable wallpaper racks at Wertheim stall. 1931. Graphite on tracing paper, 20⅜ × 29⅞" (51.8 × 75.9 cm). Mies van der Rohe Archive, gift of the architect, 1968

Lilly Reich believed that all creative design was tied to the materials and uses of the object and to the techniques with which it was made. Her work as a designer of exhibitions, of clothing and furniture, and of buildings in the Germany of the 1920s and '30s adhered to this essential criterion. Her most important role was unequivocably as an exhibition designer: for over twenty-five years, her distinctive installations allowed the materials and the content of the display to act as its primary determining features.

Reich had no formal training in design or architecture, but she learned dressmaking and various craft techniques early on, and her talent in these areas was soon recognized by a circle of women in the avant-garde design field. By 1911 Reich had earned commissions for a department store display and for the interior design and furnishings of a youth center. The event that made this career a life-long pursuit came in 1912, when she joined the Deutsche Werkbund, an organization that promoted German design through exhibitions and educational programs. Her commitment to and distinguished work for the Werkbund were deservedly rewarded in 1920, when she became the first

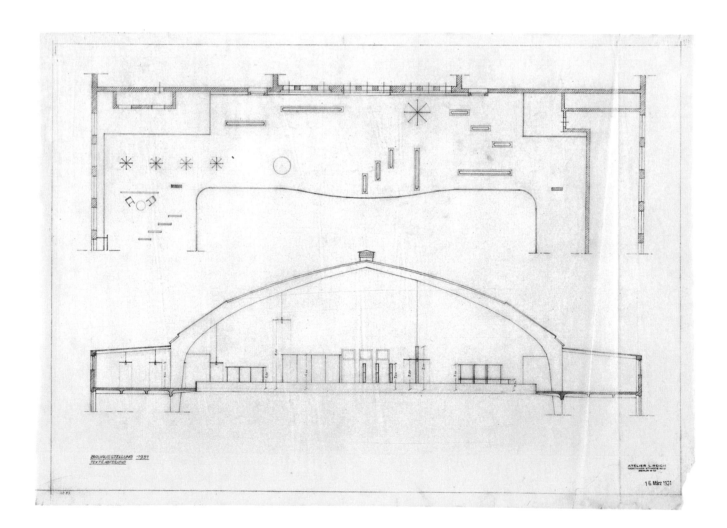

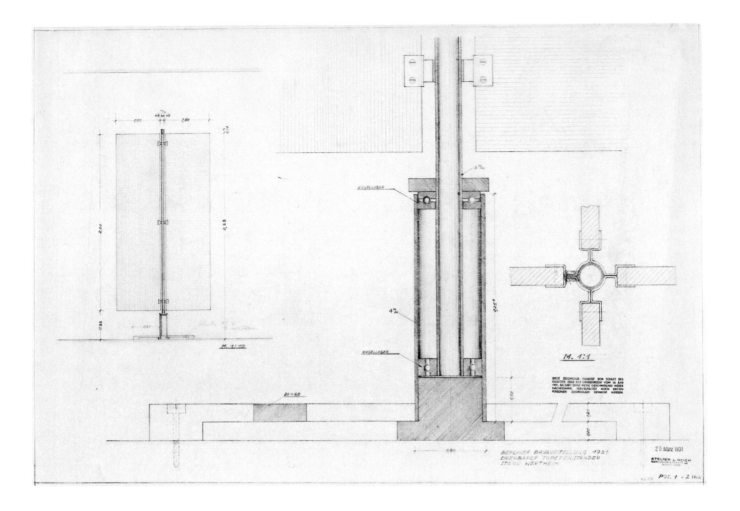

woman elected to the board of directors.

In 1927 Reich began a collaboration with Ludwig Mies van der Rohe that would last until the late 1930s. She always retained her own professional office, even when working with Mies on such large-scale and consequential projects as *The Dwelling in Our Time*. Reich participated in this exhibition as both designer and architect, and she was responsible for five full-scale installations: two apartments, a single-family house, and exhibits of exterior and interior finishing materials and furnishings. The precise

and austere drawings shown on these pages, each stamped "Atelier L. Reich," show the plan and elevation for a textile exhibit and a technical detail of a rack for a display of wallpapers. Clearly representing Reich's working process, the drawings are a construction tool rather than an end in themselves. The plan and elevation drawing for the textile exhibit also reveals the graceful, free-flowing spaces that Reich could create using only the materials of the exhibit themselves as partitions between the different sections of the display. The fabrics on show

seem to hold themselves up, with few visible signs of underlying support. This minimalist aesthetic discloses Reich's unwavering and enduring commitment to modernist principles of function and simplicity.

–Matilda McQuaid

Iakov Chernikhov
Fantasy #49: Complex Architectural Invention Project

Illustration from Chernikhov, *Arkhitekturnye fantazii* (Architectural fantasies). Book: published 1933. Drawing: before 1933. Letterpress, 12 × 8⅞" (30.5 × 22.5 cm). Arthur A. Cohen Purchase Fund, 1985

In his introduction to *Architectural Fantasies*, Iakov Chernikhov's sixth and final volume on design theory, he defended the significance of visionary paper architecture: "Not without reason, however, have great thinkers of all times accorded vast importance to fantasy, as being the forerunner of any kind of progress. To look one-sidedly at the idea of fantasy and not to consider its positive role in all fields of culture and art—this is to make a great mistake." For Chernikhov the fantasy drawing offered the architect an effective means of liberating himself from convention and imagining a future reflecting the avant-garde culture of the new Soviet Union.

As a Constructivist, and like contemporaries such as Kasimir Malevich and El Lissitzky, Chernikhov was possessed by the powers of abstraction and geometry. This is reflected in the phrase *Combination of curvilinear and rectilinear forms along principles of design*, the rather perfunctory subtitle for *Complex Architectural Invention* (drawing no. 49 from *Architectural Fantasies*): this is a formal composition based on line (curved or straight), plane, surface, body, and volume. The excitement and brilliance of

Chernikhov's fantasy lie in his dynamic handling of diagonal lines, ellipses, and bright colors, presented in a dizzying axonometric view. The imagery, unabashedly industrial in character yet devoid of any context or program, is remarkably fresh and pregnant with possibility.

In producing his *Architectural Fantasies* Chernikhov was interested not only in self-discovery but in inspiring his viewers. The seeds of his fantasies, however, never had a chance to germinate in the Soviet Union: Stalin's repressive regime, which effectively put an end to Constructivism in the 1930s, favored a banal architecture based on monumental classicism and Social Realism. The potential of *Architectural Fantasies* lay dormant until Chernikhov and other Constructivist architects were "rediscovered" in the 1980s, inspiring a new generation of architects worldwide in a movement that was labeled "deconstructivist."

—Peter Reed

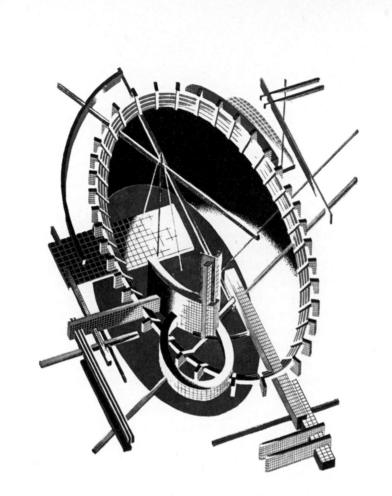

49

Архитектурное измышление усложненного типа. Объединение на конструктивных началах криволинейных форм с прямолинейными.

Oscar Nitzchke
Maison de Publicité Project, Paris, France

Elevation. Project: 1934–36. Drawing: 1936. Ink, color pencil, gouache, and graphite on lithograph on board, 28 × 20½" (71.1 × 52.1 cm). Gift of Lily Auchincloss, Barbara Jakobson, and Walter Randel, 1976

Oscar Nitzchke's Maison de Publicité was among the first architectural expressions of new forces in twentieth-century culture: advertising and the media. Nitzchke moved to Paris from Switzerland in 1920. After studying briefly at the École des Beaux-Arts, he worked in Le Corbusier's office before entering the Atelier de Bois, a progressive studio established by Auguste Perret in 1924. There he met the American architect Paul Nelson, with whom he would often work through the end of the 1930s.

The Maison de Publicité Project, which Nitzchke initiated, is his most important work of the prewar period. He designed it for a hypothetical site on the Champs Elysées, modern metropolitan Paris's bustling boulevard of cinemas and cafés. The full eighteen-meter width of the facade was to be open at street level, so that passersby could move freely into a double-height hall for media events. Massive concrete columns would support a block of advertising offices above. Beyond the hall, *boulevardières* could linger in an open-air courtyard or wander into an ovoid theater beyond, which was to play newsreels continuously.

This architectural expression of the power of the media in contemporary life was most compellingly wrought in the building's facade: in front of the glass-block windows of the advertising agencies was to hang a steel lattice that in turn would support images, logos, and other illuminated messages (to be fabricated in the building's tenth-floor workshop). Space here would be rented out, so that the images and messages would be in a constant state of flux, like the traffic on the boulevard below. As Kenneth Frampton has written of the Maison de Publicité, "Had it been built, it would have introduced a subtle rupture into the continuity of the Haussmannian avenue, replacing the *ordonnance* of the Second Empire with a pyrotechnic, kaleidoscopic field dynamically resplendent day and night."

—Terence Riley

Paul Nelson, Oscar Nitzchke, Frantz Jourdain

Palais de la Découverte Project, Paris, France

Aerial perspective. 1938. Ink, color ink, graphite, and color pencil on paper mounted on board, 28 × 28" (71.1 × 71.1 cm). Gift of the architects, 1966

Paul Nelson was the proverbial American in Paris—born in Chicago, he emigrated in around 1920 to the French capital, where he became a friend of Ernest Hemingway, Ezra Pound, and F. Scott Fitzgerald. Trying to merge his roots with his culture of adoption, he longed for an architecture that would combine American technology and energy with French humanism and sophistication. He was indeed instrumental in introducing European modern architecture to the United States, and also in bringing American flair and taste for the spectacular to France.

After taking his license at the École des Beaux-Arts in 1927, Nelson became a member of the School of Paris, the eclectic group of modernist architects that also included Robert Mallet-Stevens. His project for the Palais de la Découverte, represented in this perspective drawing, arose after the scientific exhibit at Paris's 1937 International Exposition greatly impressed authorities in the French government. As a result, Nelson and his colleagues Oscar Nitzchke and Frantz Jourdain were commissioned to produce a study for a permanent science museum in the city. The project, unfortunately never realized, envisioned a structure that was as functional as it was monumental, the outer envelope being designed to contain diverse exhibits with quite different spatial needs. Tensile cables anchored in the central ovoid shell support the circular cantilevered roof. The architects' ideals and aspirations are evident in the clear lines of the drawing, which portrays a building for a positivist, technocratic institution.

—Paola Antonelli

7

PROJET D'UN PALAIS DE LA DECOUVERTE

Nelson, Mitzschké, F.P. Jourdain
architectes - Juillet 1938

PERSPECTIVE ISOMETRIQUE

échelle 2 mm. par mètre

Ernesto Bruno La Padula
Palace of Italian Civilization, Rome, Italy

Exterior perspective, preliminary version. Project: 1936–42. Drawing: 1939.
Tempera on wood, 35 7/16 × 35 3/8" (90 × 89.9 cm). Purchase, 1984

Le Corbusier (Charles-Édouard Jeanneret)
Urban Plan for Algiers Project

Plan and perspective. Project: 1930–34. Drawing: 1935. Pastel on paper,
39¾" × 9'1½" (101 × 278.1 cm). Gift of Robert A. Jacobs, 1976

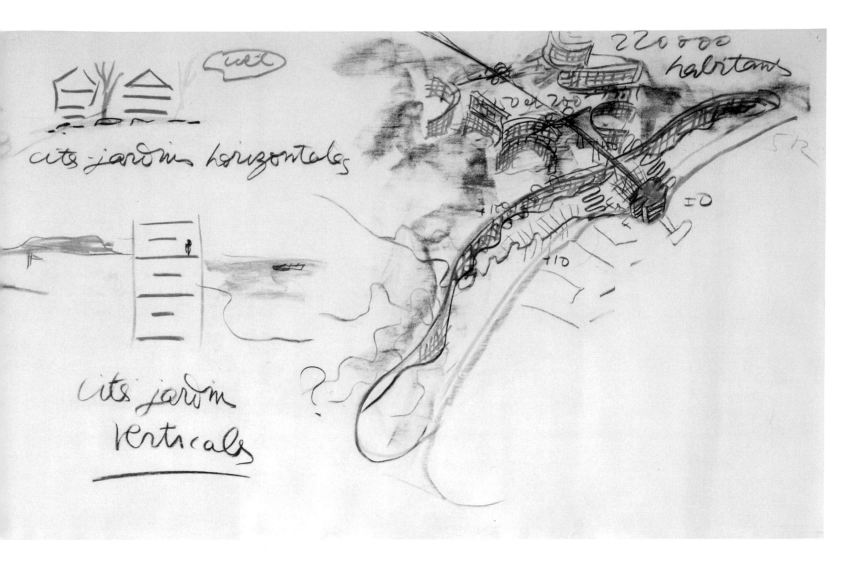

Le Corbusier made this sketch during a lecture he delivered on November 27, 1935, under the title "City Planning." He was addressing the Chicago chapter of the American Institute of Architects, as part of a lecture tour—his first trip to the United States. The trip was prompted in part by an exhibition of Le Corbusier's work at The Museum of Modern Art, organized by Philip Johnson and Henry-Russell Hitchcock.

Le Corbusier's first version of his plan for the North African city of Algiers, developed between 1930 and 1933, represented the culmination of his 1920s work on urban design, and especially of his concept of the *Ville radieuse*. Even in its several later incarnations, the plan was also a loud demonstration of the disruptive effects of his architecture, which tended to obliterate the past in order to build a better future. Well aware of this quality, the architect called his plan the "Obus" or "shrapnel" plan. It featured a business center on the docks, where the preexisting buildings were to be torn down; a residential neighborhood on the difficult, hilly site of the Fort l'Empereur; and a giant motorway, the land below it to be filled by homes for 180,000 people. The plan was as magniloquent as it was visionary, as is evident in the right half of the drawing, where Le Corbusier's blue pencil highlights the new buildings. The plan on the left shows his vision for the new city culminating in the new buildings on the docks, marked in red on a yellow field.

The courage of Le Corbusier's Obus design, his readiness to tackle urban planning on a giant scale, influenced generations of later architects and indirectly informed the construction of a number of new cities such as Brasília. As for Le Corbusier himself, however, he continued to make new proposals until 1942, but his idea for Algiers—like his other urban plans—was never built.

—Paola Antonelli

Eric Mendelsohn

Hadassah University Hospital, Mount Scopus, Jerusalem

Exterior perspective of northwest corner from University Building. Project: 1935–38. Drawing: 1935. Crayon, graphite, and gouache on sepia diazoprint, 21¼ × 22¾" (54 × 57.8 cm). Gift of Milton Scheingarten, 1972

"Look at my sketch, there is everything in it," Eric Mendelsohn once said, referring to the resemblance between his drawings and his finished works: he believed in an organic unity between drawing and building, a unity of a kind that he also saw between building and site. The distinctive sweeping lines of his drawings were intended to capture the immediate appearance of the whole. Mendelsohn's architectural ideas were shaped in the chaotic climate of Germany in the period around World War I, and most dramatically by his close association with leaders of the Expressionist movement. Even his signature style of rendering was developed during his army service in the war: tracing paper was scarce, so he began to use thumbnail sketches to portray the large complexes of his design imagination.

This early sketch for Jerusalem's Hadassah University Hospital was made in 1935, the same year Mendelsohn emigrated to Palestine. He was still working out the design, which would go through many more variations. The final complex of buildings, which includes a nursing school and a research institute as well as a hospital, stands on Mount Scopus, overlooking the ancient walled city of Jerusalem and the Moab Mountains. The drawing reveals Mendelsohn's ongoing preoccupation with the plasticity of reinforced concrete, as well as his interest in observation points affording scenic views. As this drawing shows, he was equally concerned with impressive views of the buildings from vantage points below. His consistent choice of exterior perspectives as his primary tools for describing a building, rather than the plans and elevations preferred by most modernist architects, reinforced his vision of the project as an entirety: "My sketches are data, the contour lines of an instantaneous vision. In accordance with their architectural nature, their immediate appearance is that of a whole, and this is how they must be taken."

—Matilda McQuaid

Savannah Hospital
For the University buildings.

Ludwig Mies van der Rohe
Resor House Project, Jackson Hole, Wyoming

Interior perspective of living room and south glass wall. Project: 1937–41.
Drawing: 1939. Graphite, wood veneer, cut-and-pasted gelatin silver
photographs, and cut-and-pasted photoreproduction (of Paul Klee's
Colorful Meal, 1939) on illustration board, 30 × 40" (76.2 × 101.6 cm).
Drawing attributed to George Danforth and William Priestley. Mies van der
Rohe Archive, gift of the architect, 1963

In 1937, Ludwig Mies van der Rohe accepted an invitation to visit the United States for the purpose of designing a vacation home for Mr. and Mrs. Stanley Resor near Jackson Hole, Wyoming. The house was to span a stream that branched off the Snake River; the Grand Tetons loomed in the distance. By the next year Mies had emigrated to the United States to head the architecture school at the Illinois Institute of Technology, Chicago. Although the clients had lost interest in pursuing the project, Mies continued to revise the design and created a number of new drawings, including this collage. George Danforth and William Priestley, students of Mies's, produced the collage, which represents a view from the main living area to the landscape beyond.

In preparing his original design, Mies had made sketches showing freestanding elements— a bench facing the view, a long low cabinet defining the dining space, and a taller bookcase creating a reading area. The strip of wood veneer in the collage seems to be a vestige of the cabinet, while the cutout of a painting (Paul Klee's

Colorful Meal, 1928) reflects the proportions of the bookcase. The disposition of these elements appears neither functional nor even literal, but rather suggests the flowing nature of the space Mies envisaged.

Mies had used collage as a presentation technique throughout his career, beginning with the Bismarck Monument Project of 1910. In many earlier instances he had used collage to construct more realistic views; this and other collages of the 1930s and '40s, however, are less pictorial, more evocative. Thus the photograph of the rugged mountain landscape collaged into the window frames, with cowboys on horseback, does not represent the actual view from the site but suggests what could be considered a fantasy view on the architect's part.

—Terence Riley

Ludwig Mies van der Rohe
Concert Hall Project

Interior perspective. 1942. Graphite, cut-and-pasted photoreproduction,
cut-and-pasted papers, cut-and-pasted painted paper, and gouache on
gelatin silver photograph mounted on board, 29½ × 62" (77.9 × 157.5 cm).
Studio drawing. Gift of Mrs. Mary Callery, 1963

Ludwig Mies van der Rohe
Theater Project

Combined elevation and section. 1947. Graphite, ink, cut-and-pasted papers,
and cut-and-pasted photoreproductions on illustration board, 48" × 8'
(121.9 × 243.8 cm). Studio drawing. Mies van der Rohe Archive, gift of the
architect, 1963

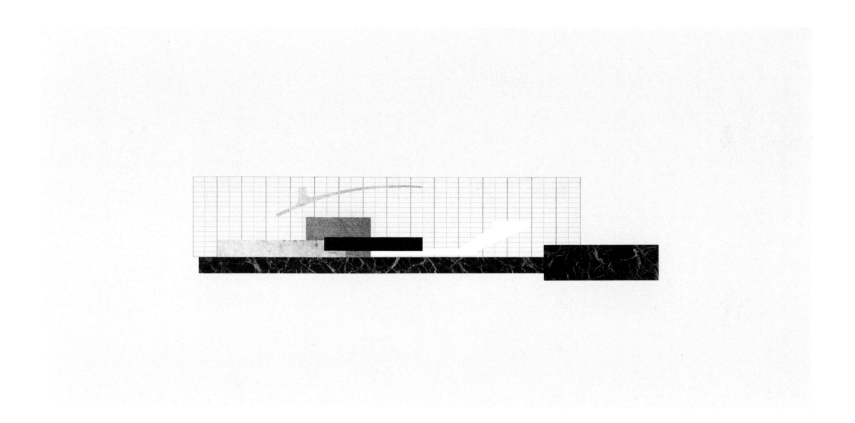

Frank Lloyd Wright

Mr. and Mrs. James Bryan Christie House, Bernardsville, New Jersey

Exterior perspective from southwest. 1940. Graphite and color pencil on tracing paper, 18 × 35½" (45.7 × 90.2 cm). Gift of Edgar Kaufmann, Jr., 1972

Mr. and Mrs. James Bryan Christie House, Bernardsville, New Jersey

Exterior perspective from east. 1940. Graphite and color pencil on paper, 18 × 35½" (45.7 × 90.2 cm). Gift of Edgar Kaufmann, Jr., 1972

VIEW FROM EAST

HOUSE FOR MR AND MRS JAMES BRYAN CHRISTIE   BERNARDSVILLE N.J.
FRANK LLOYD WRIGHT   ARCHITECT

Ludwig Mies van der Rohe

IIT Campus, Chicago, Illinois

Aerial perspective for final scheme, including the Armour Institute and surrounding buildings. Project: 1939–46. Drawing: c. 1940–41. Graphite on tracing paper, 19¼ × 29¼" (48.9 × 74.3 cm). Drawing attributed to George Danforth. Mies van der Rohe Archive, gift of the architect, 1968

Mies van der Rohe emigrated from Germany to the United States in 1938, ostensibly to take up the position of head of the architecture school at the Armour Institute of Technology, Chicago. Perhaps more important to him, though, was his understanding with the president of Armour, Henry Heald, that he would be the architect of the school's master plan for a new campus—an unprecedented opportunity for him to design an assemblage of structures in an urban center. Mies undertook preliminary studies for the campus plan between 1939 and 1941. The studies reflect the urban street grid of Chicago; in this example, a dozen or so flat-roofed two- and three-story brick buildings are arranged so that they mirror each other across 33rd Street.

While in Germany, Mies had served as the director of the Bauhaus school (from 1931 until its closing in 1933), and had taught architecture to senior students. At Armour, however—renamed the Illinois Institute of Technology (IIT) shortly after his arrival there—he taught not a master class but a curriculum patterned after the Bauhaus *Vorkurs*, preliminary courses that taught essential skills to students before they advanced to designing initially simple structures. His relationship to his IIT students, then, and their relationship to his work, were significantly different from his Bauhaus experience, and he was able to direct the students' entire architectural education from draftsmanship to urban design. In fact many of the drawings Mies produced in America, including this one, display a mixture of hands: students who had mastered his drafting style (and many of whom would eventually work in his office) would develop the base drawing to his specifications, and he would then add texture, shadow, trees, and other landscape elements to make the drawing complete.

—Terence Riley

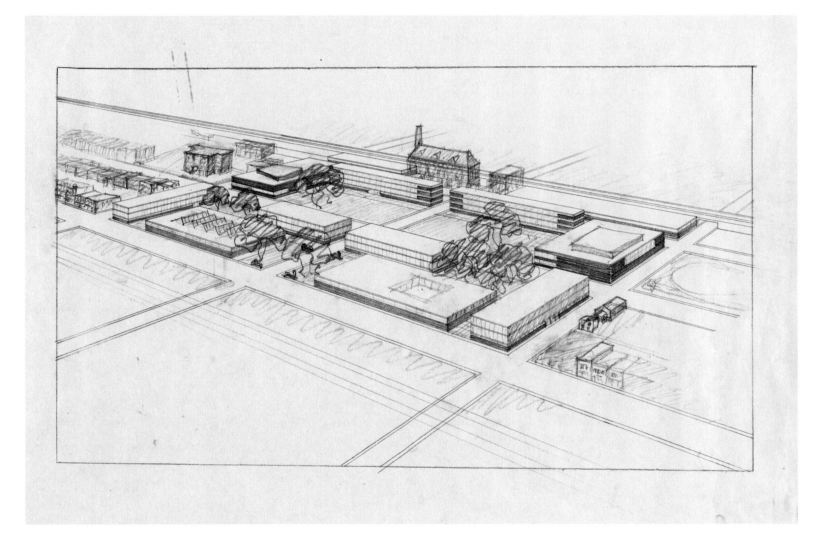

Ludwig Mies van der Rohe
Farnsworth House, Plano, Illinois

Elevation. Project: 1945–51. Drawing: 1945. Watercolor and graphite on tracing paper, 13 × 25" (33 × 63.5 cm). Drawing attributed to Edward Duckett. Later addition of watercolor: Mies van der Rohe. Mies van der Rohe Archive, gift of the architect, 1966

Philip Johnson

Preliminary Study of Glass House: Two Houses Connected by Pergola, New Canaan, Connecticut

Elevation. Project: 1945–49. Drawing: 1945. Graphite on tracing paper, 14 × 20¼" (35.6 × 51.4 cm) (irreg.). Gift of the architect, 1976

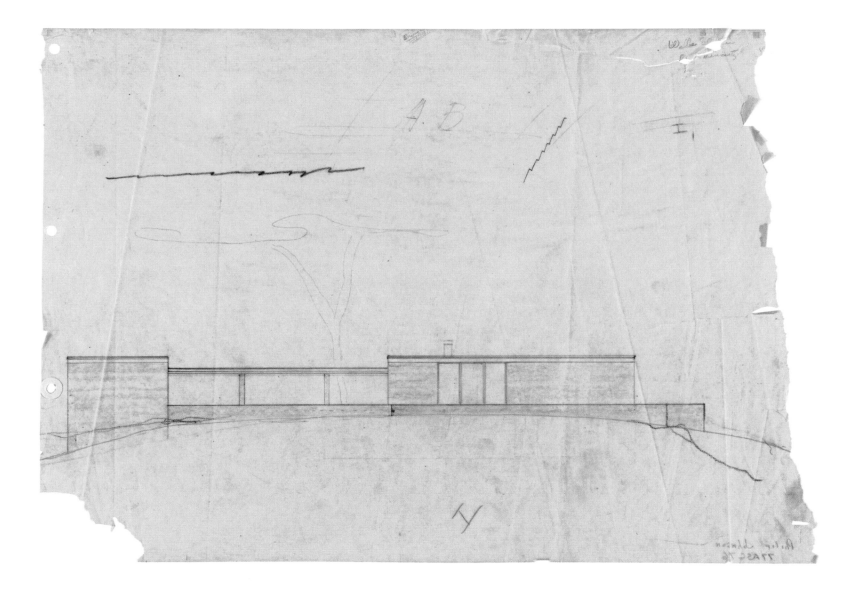

Paul Rudolph
Finney Guest House Project, Siesta Key, Florida

Aerial perspective. Project: 1947–49. Drawing: 1949. Ink and printed polymer sheet on paper, 25½ × 18⅞" (64.8 × 47.9 cm). Gift of the architect, 1989

The most popular architectural form for expressing twentieth-century modernist principles was the house. Its relatively small scale and standard program allowed and even inspired architects to experiment with architectural components such as material and spatial articulation, even while retaining the original function as shelter.

Paul Rudolph's exploration of the house began when he was a student at Harvard University's Graduate School of Design. Following the teaching of Walter Gropius, Rudolph followed the formal and structural principles of the International Style, which included clarity, a strict adherence to function, and an unambiguous expression of individual parts. These guiding principles are instrumental in his design of the Finney Guest House, an unbuilt project in South Florida. He began studies for the house in 1947, while he was still a student, then continued to work on it until around 1949. In this impeccably rendered drawing, Rudolph clearly communicates not only his design ideas for the guest house but also the reason for the drawing itself, which is "always to

inform the act of building." Choosing wood and glass as his primary material palette, Rudolph carefully arranges rectangular roof and floor planes into a spatial composition suspended above the water and surrounding landscape. The glazed walls, penetrated by indirect and filtered light, would almost allow one to feel that one was in the landscape rather than indoors, a quality in which they recall other glass houses designed several years earlier by Ludwig Mies van der Rohe and Philip Johnson.

Rudolph later came to find International Style dicta wanting, feeling that they did not fully consider the psychological aspect of space—how individuals use and inhabit it. The function of a space, he would argue, varies with each person, so that his buildings became "perpetual statements on the nature of architecture"—for him, "a continuing, ever-integrating, altering, deepening enigma."

—Matilda McQuaid

Roberto Burle Marx
Garden Design Project for Beach House for Mr. and Mrs. Burton Tremaine, Santa Barbara, California

Site plan. 1948. Gouache on board, 50¼ × 27¾" (127.6 × 70.5 cm).
Gift of Mrs. Burton Tremaine, 1966

Roberto Burle Marx was the first Brazilian landscape artist to depart from the classical principles of garden design, introducing asymmetrical plans that have influenced landscape artists around the world, as has his use of native vegetation, colorful pavements, and free-form bodies of water. His knowledge and cultivation of myriad species of plants have been cornerstones of his designs; by choosing plants that would naturally thrive in the climate of the site, and by including evergreens and perennials, Burle Marx has produced gardens that are easy to maintain and in keeping with the concepts of modern living.

Burle Marx is a painter by training, and his designs, with their careful juxtapositions of contrasting colors, shapes, and textures, have been likened to paintings, or living works of art. In his gouache plan for the Burton Tremaine Beach House, interlocking amoebic shapes curve sinuously, filling the landscape with an abstract rhythmic design. Whimsical and somewhat reminiscent of Surrealist compositional forms, they evoke the work of Jean Arp, Alexander Calder, and Joan Miró. An aspect of Burle Marx's gardens that cannot appear in the plan is their sculptural, three-dimensional quality; the flowerbeds that appear in this drawing might typically have been elevated and tiered.

The drawing also shows Burle Marx working to integrate landscape design and architecture, making the focal point of the composition the Tremaine Beach House, designed by Oscar Niemeyer. By enclosing the house in glass walls, Niemeyer erased the visual barrier between interior and exterior, bringing the garden and ocean views inside. Brise-soleils—"sun-breakers," or screens—along these walls permit privacy and easy control of light without obstructing the views outside. Oddly, neither Niemeyer nor Burle Marx had visited the California site when they prepared their plan; they worked from photographs sent to them in Brazil. Perhaps this intensified the dialogue between them, resulting in a unified aesthetic. The two men had earlier collaborated with Le Corbusier on the Ministry of Education and Public Health Building in Rio de Janeiro (1936–43), and Le Corbusier's rational architecture had in general been a departure point for Niemeyer. In the Tremaine Beach House, however, he broke away from Le Corbusier's tightly geometric curves toward the less restrictive, more free-form architecture for which he is known. Burle Marx and Niemeyer went on to work on several later collaborations, including the Ibirapuera Park Project, São Paulo (p. 107).

—Luisa Lorch

Garden by, ROBERTO BURLE MARX

Oscar Niemeyer

Beach House Project for Mr. and Mrs. Burton Tremaine, Santa Barbara, California

Exterior perspective, view toward north elevation. 1948. Ink on paper, 19 × 29" (48.3 × 73.7 cm). Gift of Mr. and Mrs. Burton Tremaine, 1966

Beach House Project for Mr. and Mrs. Burton Tremaine, Santa Barbara, California

Plan of first floor and garden. 1948. Ink on paper, 19 × 29" (48.3 × 73.7 cm). Gift of Mr. and Mrs. Burton Tremaine, 1966

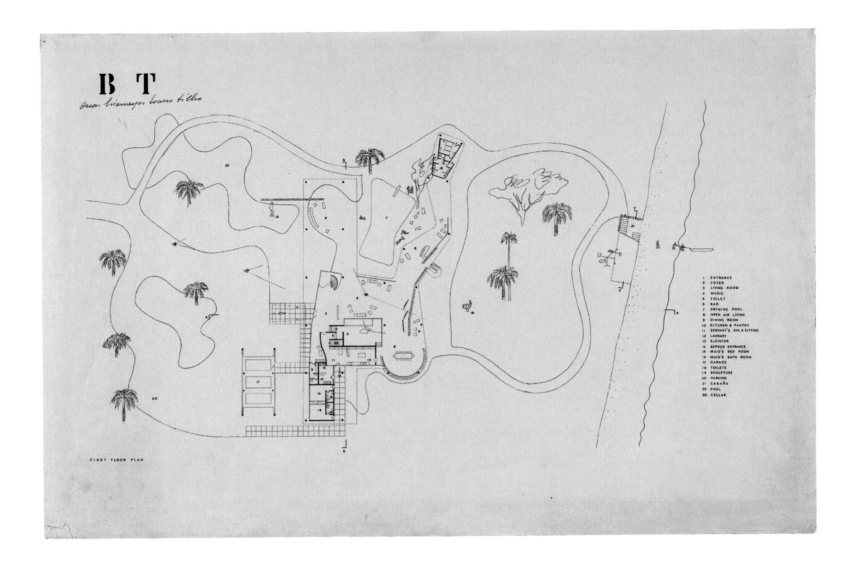

B T

Oscar Niemeyer Soares Filho

1 ENTRANCE
2 FOYER
3 LIVING ROOM
4 MUSIC
5 TOILET
6 BAR
7 SWIMING POOL
8 OPEN AIR LIVING
9 DINING ROOM
10 KITCHEN & PANTRY
11 SERVANT'S DIN. & SITTING
12 LAUNDRY
13 ELEVATOR
14 SERVICE ENTRANCE
15 MAID'S BED ROOM
16 MAID'S BATH ROOM
17 GARAGE
18 TOILETS
19 SCULPTURE
20 PARKING
21 CASAÑA
22 POOL
23 CELLAR

FIRST FLOOR PLAN

Oscar Niemeyer with United Nations Headquarters Board of Design and Wallace K. Harrison, Director of Planning

Proposal for United Nations Headquarters (Scheme 32), New York City, New York

Perspective, plan, and axonometric. Project: 1947–53. Drawing: 1947. Ink on tracing paper, 19½ × 37¾" (49.5 × 95.9 cm). Gift of Hester Diamond, 1988

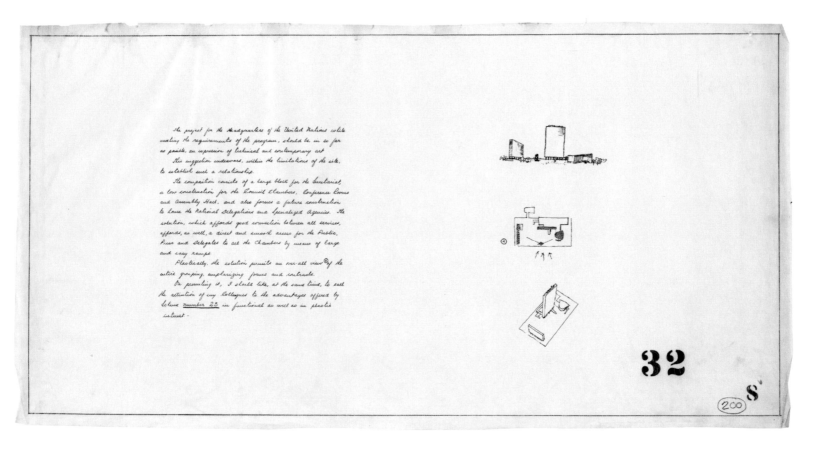

Roberto Burle Marx

Ibirapuera Park Project, São Paulo, Brazil

Site plan. 1953. Gouache and graphite on board, 39½ × 59½"
(100.3 × 151.1 cm). Gift of Roblee McCarthy, Jr., Fund and Lily
Auchincloss Fund, 1991

PLATE 17·

Frederick Kiesler

Endless House Project

Plan. Project: 1950–60. Drawing: 1951. Ink on paper with color ink on
polymer sheet overlay, 14¾ × 17⅛" (37.5 × 45.4 cm). Purchase, 1966

Endless House Project

Study for Color Clock. Project: 1950–60. Drawing: 1951. Ink and gouache
on paper, 14¾ × 18" (37.5 × 45.7 cm). Purchase, 1966

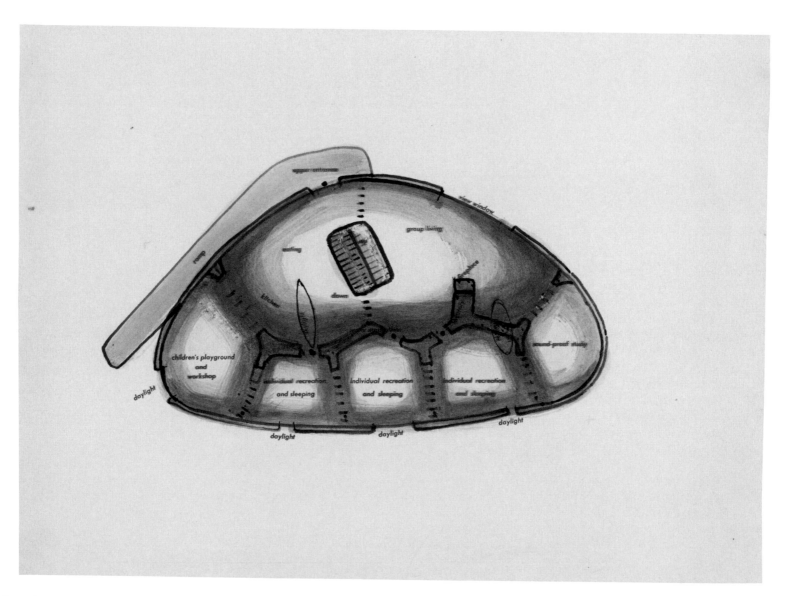

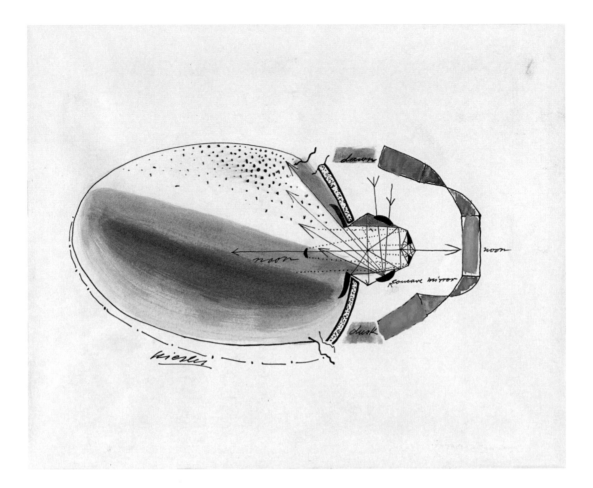

Frederick Kiesler, architect, set designer, artist, and philosopher, began to explore a new kind of "endless" architectural space in 1922 and continued to develop this theme throughout the rest of his life. The biomorphic Endless House was Kiesler's vision of a free-form, continuous, human-centered living space synthesizing painting, sculpture, architecture, and the environment. Designed in direct opposition to the static, rectilinear rooms of the sterile glass boxes that were beginning to dominate modern architecture in the 1950s, his house was to be "endless like the human body—there is no beginning and no end." For him this womblike form was akin to the female body; others have seen an egg or even the human heart, with the rooms as aortic chambers.

Kiesler's house was to provide for a healthy, comfortable, spiritually nourished existence and to promote an "exuberant" life. Raised on columns and accessible by stairs or a large curving ramp,

the visionary house is formed out of reinforced concrete, a medium permitting curving walls with irregular openings for windows and skylights. Because Kiesler felt sharp angles were artificial, the floors slope up at the edges of the rooms to form the walls, then slope inward again to create the ceiling, in a continuous line echoing the rounded shape of the house itself. The interior was to be a mélange of materials, with floors of pebbles, sand, wood, grass, and tile. Bathing pools were to replace traditional bathtubs, and frescoes and sculpture were to fill the space. While the house was to have a unified interior, the plan was versatile; flexible dividers would accommodate "every possible movement its inhabitants could make within it."

The plan consists of two parts; a floor plan in ink on paper and an acetate overlay with features of the house indicated in red. Kiesler used this technique for nine of the twenty-three drawings of

the Endless House in the collection. The overlay enabled him to maintain an interest in the amorphous shape of the house while at the same time instilling it with an architectural program.

Kiesler's house was also to incorporate a lighting system designed to serve more practical needs. A study for the Color Clock, both eye- and beetlelike, illustrates a crystalline structure of mirrors and lenses set into the roof. As the sun's rays passed through this structure, their color would gradually change, so that the house's occupant would be able to tell the time by the hue of the light. Thus the inside of the house would become the interior of an everchanging sculpture, and time would appear as a continuous flow instead of a mechanical series of segments.

—Bevin Cline

Richard Neutra

Miller House, Norristown, Pennsylvania

Exterior perspective of entrance. Project: c. 1953–56. Drawing: c. 1955.
Pastel, color pencil, and graphite on tracing paper, 16 × 25⅝" (40.6 ×
65.6 cm). Gift of Dr. and Mrs. Frank L. Miller, 1985

Eero Saarinen

**Massachusetts Institute of Technology
Auditorium and Chapel, Cambridge,
Massachusetts**

Studies for the chapel spire. Project: 1950–55. Drawing: c. 1950–55.
Ink on paper, 11 × 8½" (27.9 × 21.6 cm). Gift of Aline Saarinen, 1966

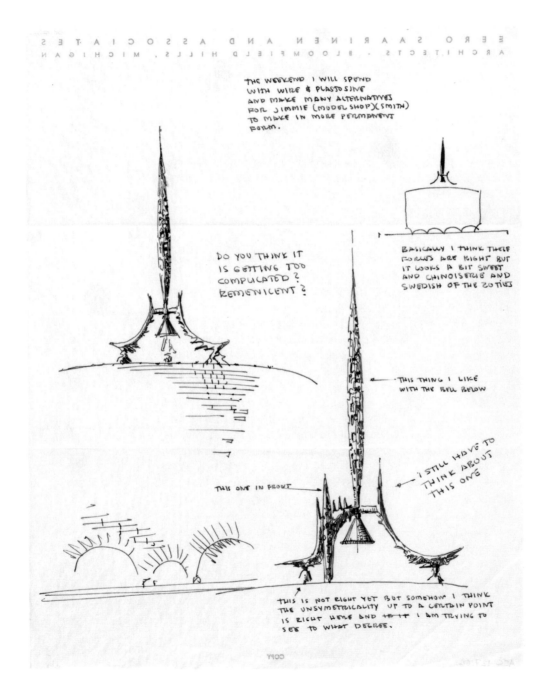

Louis I. Kahn
Traffic Study Project, Philadelphia, Pennsylvania

Plan of proposed traffic-movement pattern. Project: 1951–53. Drawing: 1952. Ink, graphite, and cut-and-pasted papers on paper, 24½ × 42¾" (62.2 × 108.6 cm). Gift of the architect, 1964

"What spaces, what activities, what buildings form the creative center of human communication?" This probing philosophical question, posed in 1955 by the American architect Louis I. Kahn, underlies the extraordinarily powerful buildings and projects for which he is known, as well as these two studies of Philadelphia's city center. In the 1950s Kahn had relatively little real work. Philadelphia, where he lived nearly all his life, was launching a decade of immense redevelopment, and Kahn was at the forefront. His numerous studies, many of them made independently without a commission, focused on the historic center city. These visionary drawings are significant not as blueprints for Philadelphia's redevelopment but because they reveal forms and ideas fulfilled in Kahn's later masterpieces.

The Traffic Study is a carefully ordered conceptual plan in which Kahn proposed a new traffic pattern. In an effort to untangle traffic congestion and to mitigate the haphazard proliferation of parking lots that plagued postwar American cities, Kahn reordered the streets according to a functional hierarchy. Like an idiosyncratic musical score, the drawing's abstract notational system corresponds to different tempos of traffic, such as the stop-and-go movement of trucks and buses (dotted lines), the fast flow of vehicles around the periphery (arrows), and the stasis of cars in parking garages (spirals). To explain his movement study, Kahn invoked a historical analogy: for him, the girdle of expressways and parking towers circling the city center metaphorically recalled the walls and towers that protected the medieval cities of Europe. Kahn's specific comparison was to the largely medieval town of Carcassonne, in the South of France: just as Carcassonne was a city built for defense, Kahn envisioned the modern city center having to defend itself against the automobile.

In the small bird's-eye panorama (p. 114) Kahn further developed his idea of a city surrounded by massive cylindrical parking towers defending the center—which he now called the "Forum"—from the onslaught of automobiles and the forces of decentralization that threatened human interaction. The historicism that was beginning to emerge in his work is evinced by the gateway towers, which explicitly recall ancient monuments such as the Roman Colosseum in various states of decay. Kahn's idealized drawing was clearly inspired by Piranesi's famous eighteenth-century views of Rome and imaginary buildings. Here, buildings in a variety of archetypal geometric forms populate the city center. Kahn believed that only by a centralization of buildings and activities, supported by a clear ordering of streets and traffic, would meaningful urban life be preserved.

—Peter Reed

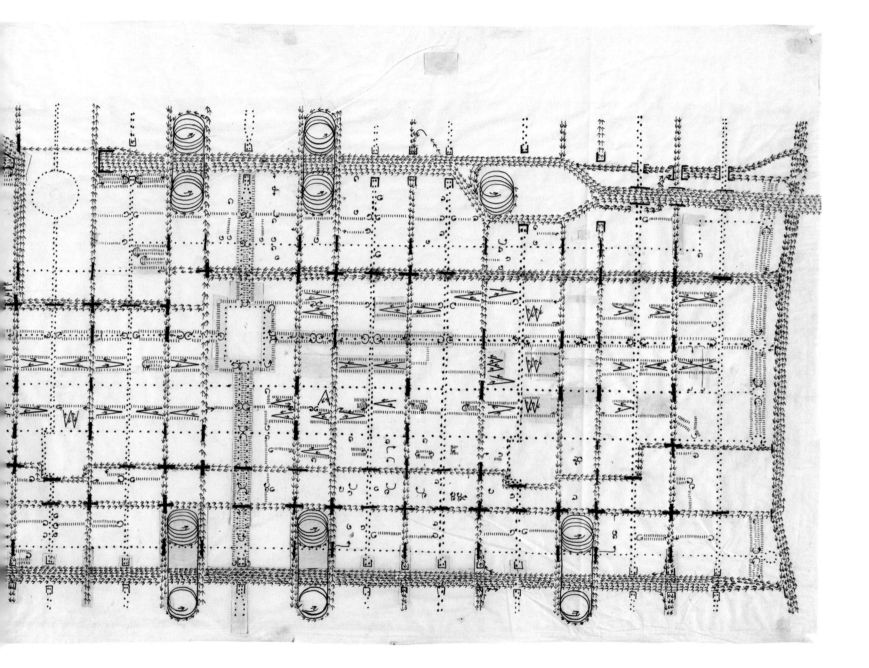

Louis I. Kahn

Civic Center Project, Philadelphia, Pennsylvania

Aerial perspective. Project: 1956–57. Drawing: 1957. Ink on tracing paper,
11 × 14" (27.9 × 35.6 cm). Gift of the architect, 1964

Travel Sketch for Sainte Cécile Cathedral, Albi, France

Exterior perspective. 1959. Ink on paper, 10⅜ × 8¼" (26.4 × 20.9 cm).
Gift of the architect, 1964

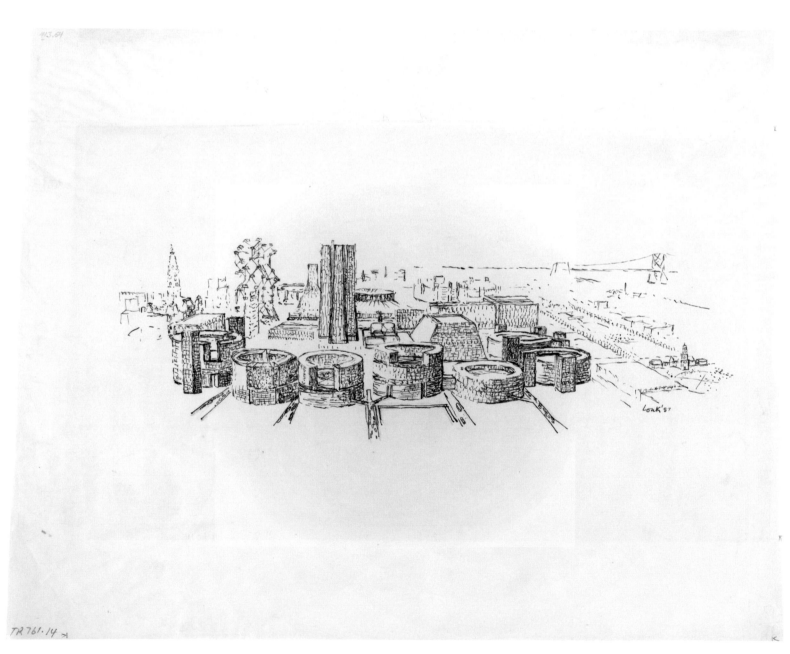

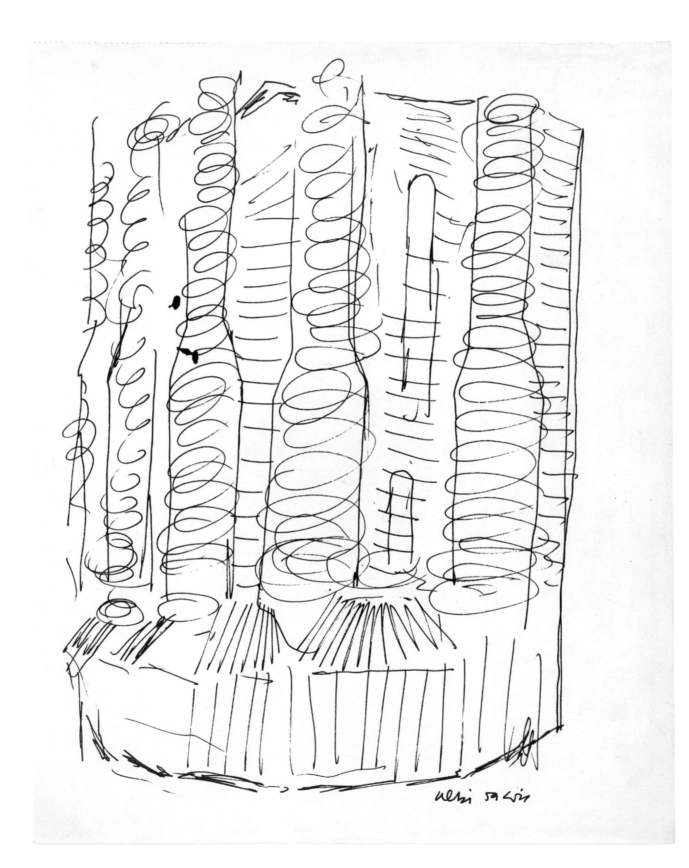

Louis I. Kahn

Alfred Newton Richards Medical Research Building and Biology Building, University of Pennsylvania, Philadelphia, Pennsylvania

Plans and elevations of service towers, preliminary version. Project: 1957–65. Drawing: 1957. Crayon, graphite, and color pencil on tracing paper, 12 × 20¼" (30.5 × 51.4 cm). Gift of the architect, 1967

Alfred Newton Richards Medical Research Building and Biology Building, University of Pennsylvania, Philadelphia, Pennsylvania

Exterior perspective, final version. Project: 1957–65. Drawing: 1960. Graphite on tracing paper, 23 × 23½" (58.4 × 59.7 cm). Gift of the architect, 1967

When The Museum of Modern Art exhibited the Richards Medical Research Building, in 1961, the show's curator, Wilder Green, described it as "probably the single most consequential building constructed in the United States since the war. It is simultaneously a building and a manifesto." Reacting against the Miesian concept of "universal space," Kahn's design for his alma mater, where he also taught architecture, integrates structure, space, and mechanical elements precisely and expressively within a compositional whole. These two drawings illustrate different stages of the design process: one of them is rife with preliminary sketches in Kahn's own hand; the later, perspective rendering shows the building's final design around the time of its completion. (The Biology Building, seen on the right of the drawing, was built subsequently.)

A chief concept in the design is what Kahn called "served and servant spaces." This implicit functional hierarchy is evident in the massing and overall structure depicted in the perspective: the windowed laboratory towers (the "served" spaces) are abutted by exterior stair towers and mechanical stacks faced in brick (the "servant" spaces). This clear distinction of functions led Kahn to celebrate the elaborate exhaust system

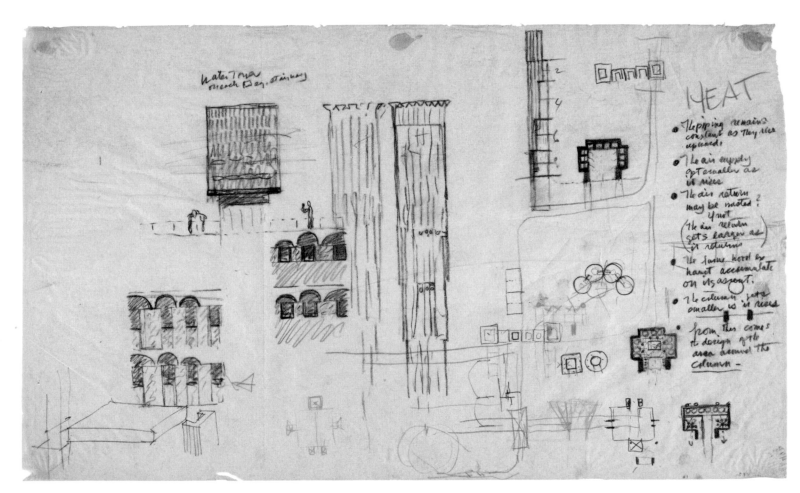

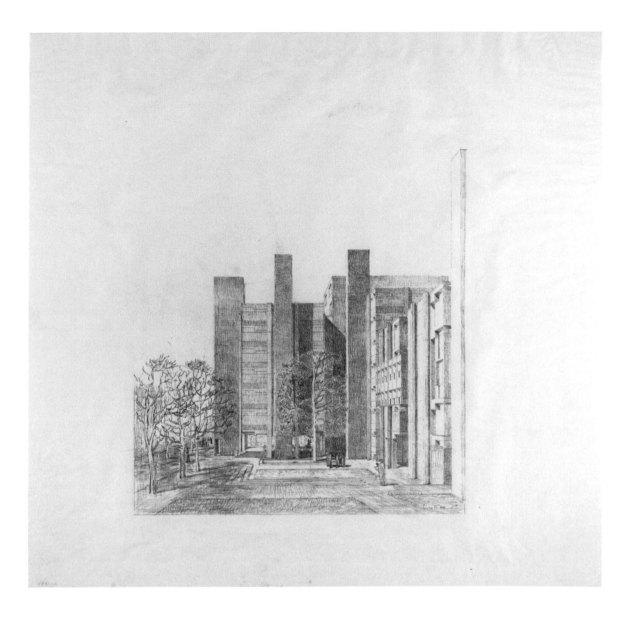

(necessary to replace fumes from the labs with breathable air). The preliminary sketches and annotations record Kahn's thought process as he explored the concepts and forms of the columns and towers, their interstitial spaces, and the structural system. In this tentative group of drawings, the chimney towers grow wider at the top to accommodate the increasing number of flues (clusters of circles) added at each floor. In the final version, developed with the structural engineer August Komendant, Kahn eliminated the towers' picturesque stepped profile in favor of a

more simplified skyline. Similarly, on the left side of the sheet, he explored the ingenious concrete structural system, focusing on the lunette windows wedded to a cantilevered beam directly above them: the windows increase in size toward the end of the beam. In the final solution, the tapering beam and windows were further refined and given a rectangular shape.

The towers recall the medieval Italian town of San Gimignano, which Kahn had studied in early drawings, and also fit harmoniously with the building's collegiate neo-Gothic neighbors. More

significantly, however, the project reinvigorated modern architecture by expanding the idea of functionalism. Dissatisfied with modernism's steel and glass aesthetic, which had become clichéd, Kahn developed an approach that reflected his beaux-arts training and love of architectural history without facile historicizing.

—Peter Reed

Michael Webb (Archigram)
**Furniture Manufacturers Association
Headquarters Project, High Wycombe, England**
Side elevation. 1958. Graphite and ink on tracing paper mounted on board,
23½ × 32" (59.7 × 81.3 cm). Gift of The Howard Gilman Foundation, 2000

Michael Webb was one of the founding members of Archigram, the radical architecture group that dominated the British design scene during the 1960s and early 1970s. The group has proven prescient: the fluid, mobile cities plugged into worldwide communications networks that they imagined in the 1960s were in many respects realized before the end of the century.

This drawing predates the group's founding, in 1960–Webb produced it while he was still a student at London's Regent Street Polytechnic. Other drawings for the project were featured in the Museum's *Visionary Architecture* exhibition of 1960, which examined a group of extraordinary futuristic designs, ranging from studies well into the developmental phase to outright fantasies and imaginings. The technical aspects of the Furniture Manufacturers Association Headquarters, and specifically the use of precast concrete, were central to the building's design, which was motivated by Webb's interest in the work of the Italian engineer Pier Luigi Nervi. The lower floors were to hold the association's offices and an auditorium, at left, poised and cantilevered by a ramp; the spaces on the upper floors were to be leased out to various companies. Wherever feasible, the offices were to be precast-concrete cells, to be hoisted by crane and inserted into a skeleton frame. The careful articulation of the tubular passageways and elevator shafts and the bulbous auditorium provides a contrast to the orthogonal forms of the offices and showrooms and clearly anticipates Renzo Piano and Richard Rogers's Centre Pompidou, Paris, designed over a decade later.

—Matilda McQuaid

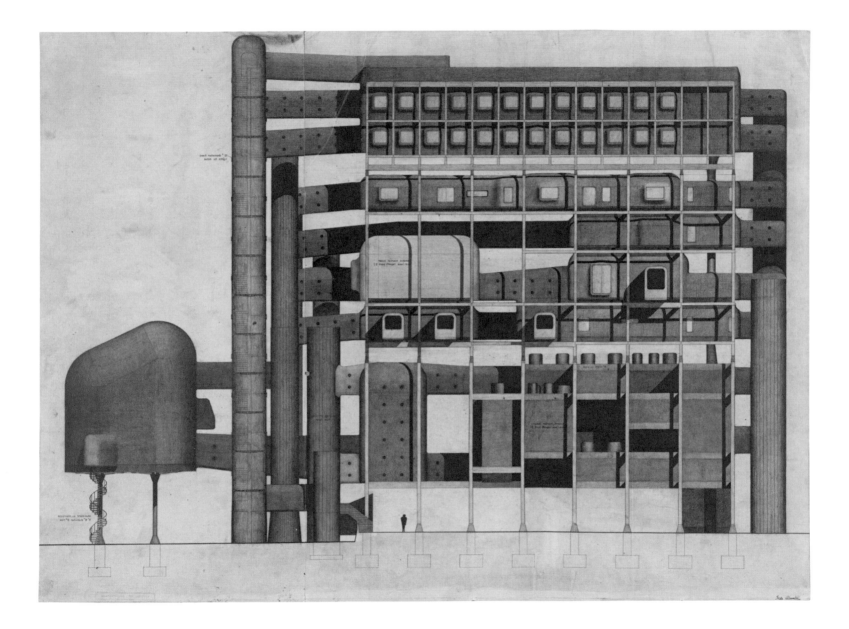

Arata Isozaki

City in the Air Project, Shinjuku, Tokyo, Japan

Elevation. Project: 1960–61. Drawing: 1960. Ink and color pencil on paper, 20⅞ × 33¾" (53 × 85 cm). Gift of The Howard Gilman Foundation, 2000

Arata Isozaki began his career in 1954, in the office of Kenzo Tange, his former professor and the most influential figure in postwar Japanese architecture. While Tange's architecture was in itself radical in its conception, it was his urban projects that most influenced the younger generation of architects, including Isozaki. Tange's Plan for Tokyo (1960) is critical in this regard. Trying to reconcile the incredible density of Tokyo's urban fabric with the rapid expansion and reformulation of modern social structures, Tange's plan proposed multilevel urban construction layered over the existing city and its waterways.

Radical new visions of the city were not limited to Tange's plans for Tokyo. The New Babylon project that Constant Nieuwenhuis began in the 1950s, Yona Friedman's Spatial Plan for Paris of 1958, and the work of the collective Archigram in the 1960s embraced urban transformation as a means toward achieving social change. In Isozaki's City in the Air Project of 1960–61, the multilayered city hovers over the traditional city, the scale of which can be seen at the far right. Highways and parking structures thread their way between massive pylons that support blocks of offices and apartments above. The ground plane is reconstituted as tiers of gardens above and within the blocks.

Isozaki's City in the Air Project was undertaken in 1960, the same year a number of younger architects, almost all of them affiliated with Tange, issued the Metabolist Manifesto. While Isozaki was never formally a member of the group, his project and the work produced by the Metabolists over the course of the decade largely reflected Tange's description of his own urban work: "By incorporating elements of space, speed, and drastic change in the physical environment, we created a method of structuring having elasticity and changeability."

—Terence Riley

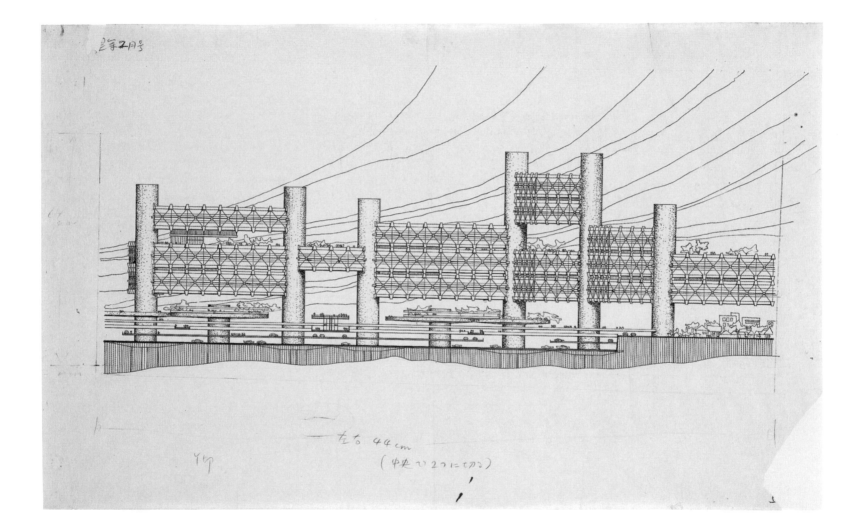

Eero Saarinen
Terminal Building, Dulles International Airport, Sterling, Virginia

Exterior perspective. c. 1958–63. Graphite on tracing paper, 18 × 34½"
(45.7 × 87.6 cm). Gift of Aline Saarinen, 1966

Eero Saarinen intended his Dulles International Airport Terminal to evoke both the monumentality of a federal building in the nation's capital—the airport serves the Washington, D.C., metropolitan area—and the dynamism of the dawning age of jet travel. (Dulles was the first commercial airport designed for jet aircraft from the start.) Consistent with various kinds of modernist architecture, the form of the structure was to convey its function, its sweeping lines rising visually from the horizontal plane of the site.

Son of the Finnish architect Eliel Saarinen, Eero Saarinen had briefly studied sculpture in Paris before attending the Yale School of Architecture. In this drawing for the terminal, the concrete roof slab and piers thrust upward as if to take flight. It is Saarinen's use of foreshortening—there is dramatic differentiation of size between the front of the slab and the back—that gives the mass this dynamic sense of liftoff and speed. In actuality the roof of the terminal was to be suspended like a hammock between two rows of columns, 65 feet high in the front and 40 in the back, creating a grand interior space 600 feet long. In order to reduce the distances that passengers had to walk, and to create a compact building, Saarinen developed "mobile lounges," motorized departure lounges on wheels that would detach from the terminal and transport travelers to their aircraft, located at service areas near the runways.

Between 1958 and 1962 Saarinen was also designing another important airport terminal, the TWA building at Idlewild (now John F. Kennedy) Airport. This sculptural building also expresses its function, appearing not to hover but to be caught in mid-flight. Both buildings demonstrate Saarinen's belief that architecture can be seen as placing something between earth and sky.

—Bevin Cline

Paul Rudolph

Arthur W. Milam Residence, Ponte Vedra Beach, Florida

Exterior perspective from beach. Project: 1960–62. Drawing: c. 1960–62.
Ink on board, 33 × 30" (83.8 × 76.2 cm). Gift of the architect, 1985

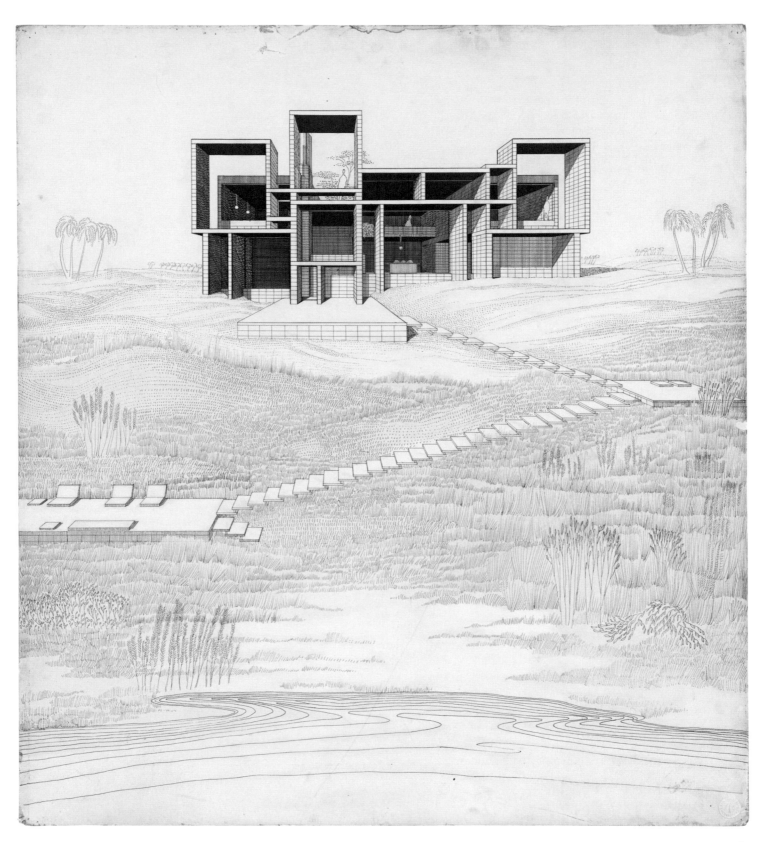

Louis I. Kahn

Salk Institute for Biological Studies, La Jolla, California

Elevation of Laboratory and Meeting House. Project: 1959–65. Drawing: 1962. Laboratory completed in 1965; Meeting House unbuilt. Charcoal on tracing paper, 23¾" × 9'1½" (60.3 × 278.1 cm). Gift of the architect, 1964

Aplace he could invite Picasso—this is how the scientist Jonas Salk, developer of the polio vaccine, described his dream for a new laboratory complex when he first met Louis Kahn to discuss the program. Salk wanted a place where scientists, humanists, and artists could work together toward a greater understanding of life's processes.

This panoramic elevation, rendered in Kahn's favorite medium of charcoal on yellow tracing paper, portrays the final version of the Institute on its dramatic site: an expansive, irregular landscape on coastal bluffs overlooking the Pacific Ocean. On the right or eastern edge, amid a grove of trees, low-lying laboratories hug the land. On the western edge of the site the so-called Meeting House perches on the bluff. Inspired in part by his admiration of medieval monasteries and cloisters, Kahn envisioned this complex as a kind of forum for social and intellectual interaction.

Kahn's monochromatic rendering is well suited to convey the qualities of his favored construction material of poured-in-place concrete. One can discern some of the buildings' details: the scientists' individual studies, the stair towers punctuating the long laboratories, the idiosyncratic screen walls with their lunettes. But more significant is the drawing's sense of monumentality and awe. The Salk Institute is an inspired realm, and one of Kahn's finest works. Here this deeply philosophical architect not only created a place reflecting the interdependence of the scientific and the humanistic disciplines but seems to have satisfied his lifelong ambition to give shape to the unmeasurable.

—Peter Reed

Yona Friedman
Spatial City Project

Aerial perspective. Project: 1958–59. Drawing: 1958. Ink on tracing paper,
8⅜ × 10¾" (21.3 × 27.3 cm). Gift of The Howard Gilman Foundation, 2000

Born and schooled in Budapest, active in Haifa until 1957 and later in Paris, Yona Friedman, like many of his contemporaries, has concentrated on the scale of the city as it has evolved. His proposed ideal architecture is open in character, as this drawing for his Spatial City Project shows. The Spatial City is a unit that can be repeated ad infinitum. All of the structural elements connected to the individual user, such as walls, floor slabs, and partitions, are radically mobile, and the architecture deliberately avoids committing itself to any particular style or pattern of use. Versatile and free as Friedman's composition is, however, it is contained by a superior order, on which it relies: the wide grid of pillars and slabs on which it stands. Friedman called this grid the "spatial infrastructure," and designed it for collective use. The user's determination was to play as important a role in it as the architect's: "Mobile architecture looks for techniques which don't impose a preconceived plan. . . . It is the user who makes the project with a potential 'designer's participation.'" The design of Friedman's ideal city is only perfected in its use.

The concept of mobile architecture was Friedman's contribution to the tenth International Congress of Modern Architecture (CIAM) in Dubrovnik in 1956. It was during this session of the congress that modernism was famously called into question as an outdated, static scheme inappropriate for new global realities. Friedman's concept highlighted the relationship between social dynamics and architecture in the proto-postmodern world, and suggested to architects how they could include that relationship in their thinking about the future.

—**Paola Antonelli**

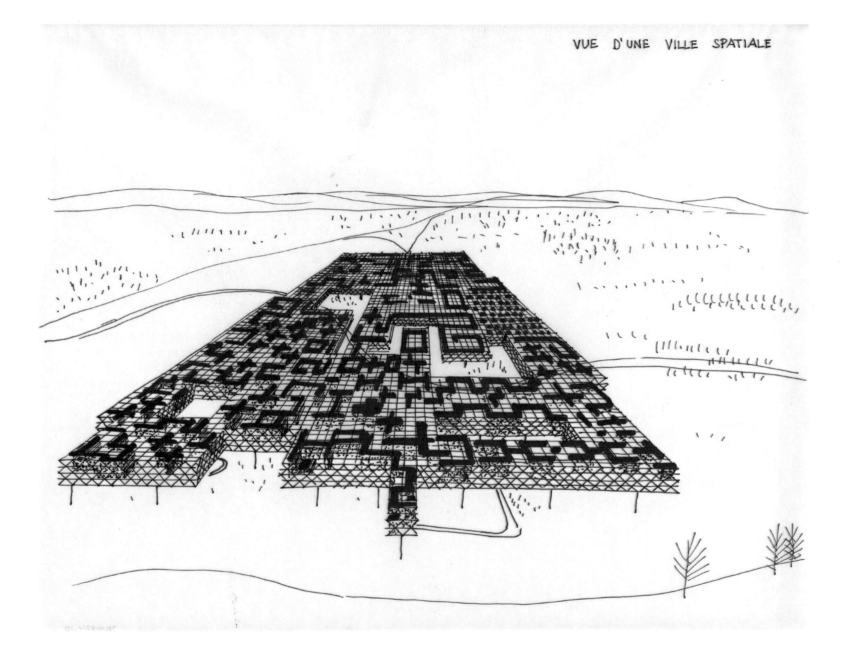

Kisho Kurokawa
Helix City Project, Tokyo, Japan

Plan. 1961. Cut-and-pasted gelatin silver photographs and ink on cut-and-pasted tracing paper on paper, 21½ × 17½" (54.6 × 44.5 cm). Gift of the architect, 1992

Kisho Kurokawa was a leading member of the Metabolist movement in Japanese architecture of the 1960s, a movement reflecting the belief that cities could be designed according to organic paradigms. Metabolist architects hoped that the use of biological processes as models would give them efficient ways to deal with the rapid growth and technological progress of societies all over the world. Their design philosophy involved gigantic buildings, of a size that Le Corbusier had envisioned and sometimes built in past decades. This monumental scale reflected operations they also saw at work in contemporary urban growth; their buildings were to become nodes in the organic fabric of the rapidly growing city. The Metabolist architect Fumihiko Maki is credited with coining the word "megastructure," in an essay of 1961; he defined it as "a large frame in which all the functions of a city or part of a city are housed . . . [the frame is] made possible by present-day technology." For the international movement of architects trying to design the ideal city of the future, "megastructure" became a key word.

Kurokawa's impressive Helix City Project envisioned an organic city plan, shown in this drawing, based on service towers connected by an infrastructure of bridges spanning both land and sea. Residential buildings would neatly fill the spaces between, and the pattern could be repeated ad infinitum. Kurokawa, who had worked with Kenzo Tange on his generative Plan for Tokyo of 1960, based his architecture "on the principle of life," he stated in 1998. More than a utopian vision, his Helix City shows an attempt to respond to the dramatic shortage of dwelling space in modern Japan by distributing the built environment in a more structured and sensible way.

—Paola Antonelli

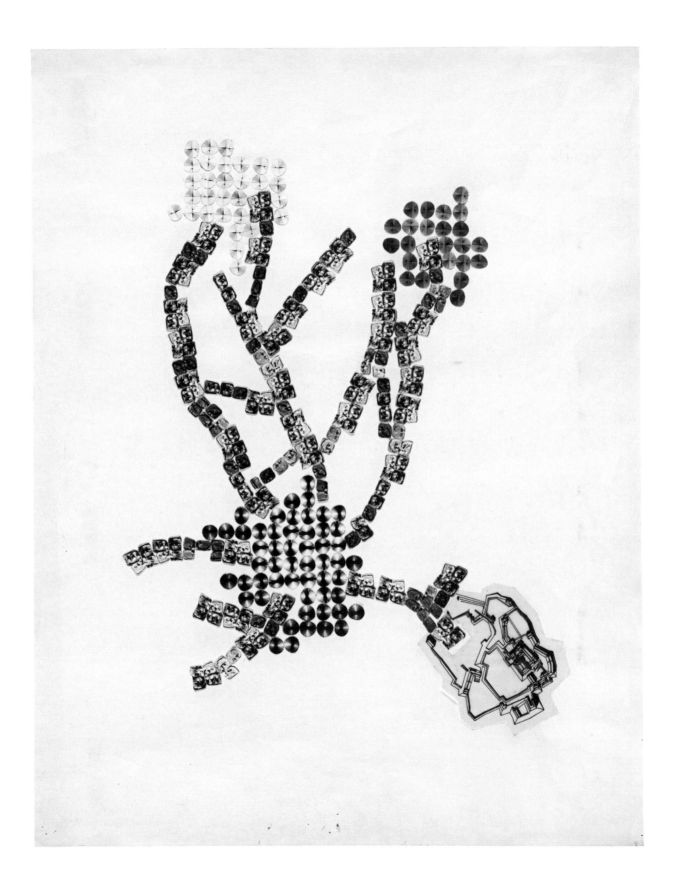

Louis I. Kahn

Mikveh Israel Synagogue Project, Philadelphia, Pennsylvania

Interior perspective. Project: 1961–72. Drawing: 1963. Charcoal on tracing paper on board, 23⅛ × 21" (58.7 × 53.3 cm). Gift of the architect, 1964

Louis I. Kahn

Sher-e-Bangla Nagar, Dhaka, Bangladesh

Perspective of hostels. Project: 1962–83. Drawing: 1963. Charcoal and
crayon on tracing paper, 18 × 20" (45.7 × 50.8 cm). Gift of the architect,
1967

Louis I. Kahn
Memorial to the Six Million Jewish Martyrs
Project, New York City, New York

Perspective of central pier. Project: 1966–72. Drawing: 1968. Charcoal and graphite on tracing paper, 44½ × 66" (113 × 167.6 cm). Purchase, 1997

What material and form could adequately express the memory of a catastrophe as unbearable as the martyrdom of 6 million Jews in the Holocaust? In 1967, on the recommendation of Philip Johnson, a committee charged with building such a memorial in New York City commissioned Louis Kahn to design it. The monument was to be situated in Battery Park, at the southern tip of Manhattan, where it would have distant views of the Statue of Liberty. Kahn proposed an abstract design: a granite pedestal supporting seven glass piers, so that, in his words, the "sun could come through and leave a shadow filled with light."

This spectacular image, the sole drawing included in an exhibition devoted to the Memorial at The Museum of Modern Art in 1968, captures the sense of transparency and reflection that Kahn envisioned through loose, energetic strokes of charcoal pencil on the luminous yellow paper.

The drawing focuses on the central glass pier, made of glass blocks etched with inscriptions in Hebrew and English, and built to contain a small circular chapel. Around this central space are the other six piers, all of them solid glass. Kahn described the immaterial quality these vitreous forms would have: "Changes of light, the seasons of the year, the play of the weather, and the drama of movement on the river will transmit their life to the monument." This structure of light embodied hope as well as despair. The project is contemporary with one of Kahn's last philosophical concepts, "silence and light," where light symbolizes the source of life and the inspiration of the creative act.

—Peter Reed

Hans Hollein
Monument to Victims of the Holocaust Project

Exterior perspective. 1963. Graphite on cut-and-pasted paper and graphite on cut-and-pasted printed paper on printed paper, 5⅞ × 11½" (14.9 × 29.2 cm). Gift of Philip Johnson, 1963

Walter Pichler
Underground Building Project

Isometric. 1963. Ink and graphite on paper, 15 × 27 ¼"
(38.1 × 69.3 cm) (irreg.). Philip Johnson Fund, 1963

Walter Pichler's exquisitely drawn projects for floating or underground buildings and cities are dreamlike images suggesting lost civilizations, long abandoned only to be discovered and rebuilt by the artist's hand. Primarily a sculptor rather than an architect, Pichler carefully constructs his architectural visions on paper or in the form of models. His practice has influenced a generation of architects and designers, including such figures as Raimund Abraham and the Coop Himmelblau firm.

Underground Building was included in the Museum's 1967 exhibition *Architectural Fantasies*, which also featured drawings by Pichler's fellow Austrians Abraham and Hans Hollein. All three were fascinated by the machine, which not only inspired them but which they took as a fundamental component of their designs. The structure in *Underground Building* resembles an ominous defensive artillery battery. It is to be imagined as the entrance to an elaborate underground metropolis, with a multitude of incisions and protruding shafts offering visual portals from which to look out or in. The building is painstakingly stratified, with Pichler using color as a construction material in the same way that he uses wood, metal, and clay to build his sculpture. Working in a palette of brown (in this drawing) or yellow, he applies a thin wash over particular areas of the drawing. The result has strength yet no obvious purpose—but for Pichler it doesn't need one, since whatever is built will find its own usefulness.

—Matilda McQuaid

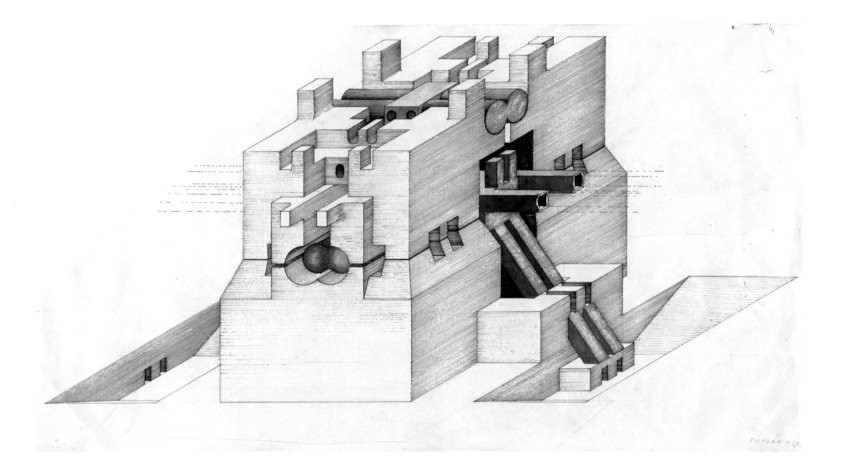

Raimund Abraham

Glacier City Project, from the Linear City Series

Sectional perspective. Project: 1963–66. Drawing: 1964. Ink and graphite on paper, 8¼ × 15⅜" (21 × 39.1 cm). Philip Johnson Fund, 1965

Universal City Project, from the Linear City Series

Aerial perspective of Earth's horizon. Project: 1963–66. Drawing: 1966. Cut-and-pasted printed papers, cut-and-pasted gelatin silver photograph, and ink on board, 13⅛ × 17" (33.3 × 43.2 cm). Purchase, 1968

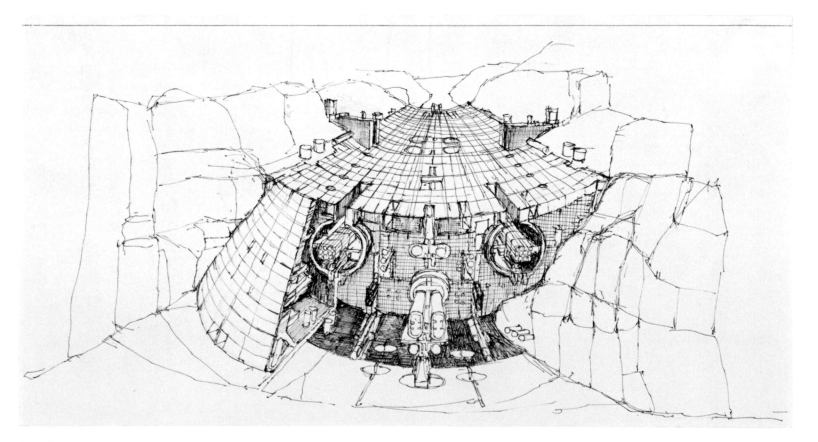

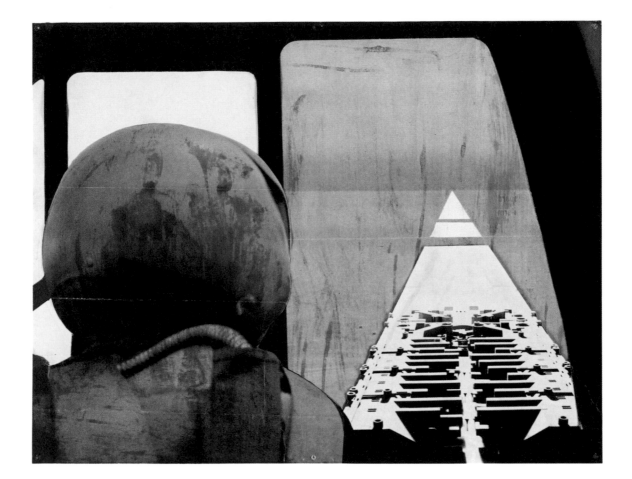

The architectural visions of Raimund Abraham describe barren landscapes, alien planets, and the dawn of a new world. Intellectual speculation is integral to the drawings, which architectural critics have called "visual poems." These two drawings from Abraham's Linear City series demonstrate his enduring fascination with the city, its eternal fluctuations and mechanistic foundations. Along with works by his fellow Austrians Walter Pichler and Hans Hollein, they were featured in the Museum's 1967 exhibition *Architectural Fantasies: Drawings from the Museum's Collection*, which focused on projects that relied on the machine not as a source of inspiration for design but as a basis for civilization.

The works conjure up images of missile sites and giant engineering installations. They are devoid of people: for Abraham, "Architectural scale can no longer be based on the physical measurement of the human body, but has to be based on the new perception media, on all the senses, on dreams." Glacier City is almost invisible in its location, between the walls of a valley and beneath a membrane suspended above it to serve as a protective shield and a collector of solar energy. The part of it we see suggests a gunboat. The city's growth in its underground cavity is horizontal and linear rather than vertical; like arteries running through a living body, streets, transportation lines, and the sewer system are the functioning architectural passages. Similarly with Universal City, we seem to gaze out of a window onto a "settlement" strip that disappears into the horizon. This megastructure or artificial valley has the potential for infinite growth and universal applicability—it could form a ring around the globe. For Abraham the horizon is an architectural site, an idea influenced by the Viennese philosopher Ernest Mach and his theory of collision: the site of collision in Abraham's work is the meeting of earth and sky.

"Building" for Abraham can mean to build with words as well as with lines, or volume, or concrete. Each is a reality, each is autonomous, and each has its own expression. As Abraham has said, "Even the principle of drawing reveals the origin of architecture—the act of interfering in, and shaping, space. For me the piece of paper is the space and the pencil the tool with which to intervene and shape."

—Matilda McQuaid

Peter Cook (Archigram)
Maximum Pressure Area, Plug-In City Project

Section. Project: 1962–64. Drawing: 1964. Ink and color ink on photomechanical print, 32⅞ × 57¹¹⁄₁₆" (83.5 × 146.5 cm). Gift of The Howard Gilman Foundation, 2000

Peter Cook's Plug-In City was one of the many vast, visionary creations to come out of the collaborative and radical British architectural group Archigram. The name of the group, according to Cook, was to be "analogous to a thing like a message or some abstract communication, telegram, aerogramme, etc." It also describes their method: architecture by drawing, rather than actual building.

Archigram were an influential architectural component of the "British invasion," the influx of British culture into the United States of the 1960s. Between 1960 and 1974 they produced nine provocative issues of their magazine, *Archigram*, and over 900 exuberant drawings illustrating imaginary architectural projects ranging in inspiration from technological developments to the counterculture, from space travel through science fiction to the Beatles. Their work directly opposed the period's functionalist architecture, which they saw as worn out; they liked to design nomadic alternatives to traditional ways of living, including walking cities and wearable houses—mobile, flexible, impermanent architectures that they hoped would be liberating. Cook believed that "architecture could break out

of its narrow-mindedness if it acquired elements (a vocabulary of form) from outside itself."

The Plug-In City was designed to span the English Channel and reach into Europe. An urban environment as a "megastructure" incorporating residences, access routes, and essential services for the inhabitants, it was intended to accommodate and encourage change through obsolescence: each building outcrop (houses, offices, supermarkets, hotels) would be removable, and a permanent "crane-way" would facilitate continual rebuilding. The life of the units would vary in length, and the main structure itself would last only forty years. The network would include a high-speed monorail, and hovercrafts would serve as moving buildings.

Cook's cheerful, colorful drawing is accessible and inviting. The comic book style popular with Archigram members, and characteristic of the counterculture of the 1960s, conveys a youthful excitement with form in a technologically enhanced world.

—Bevin Cline

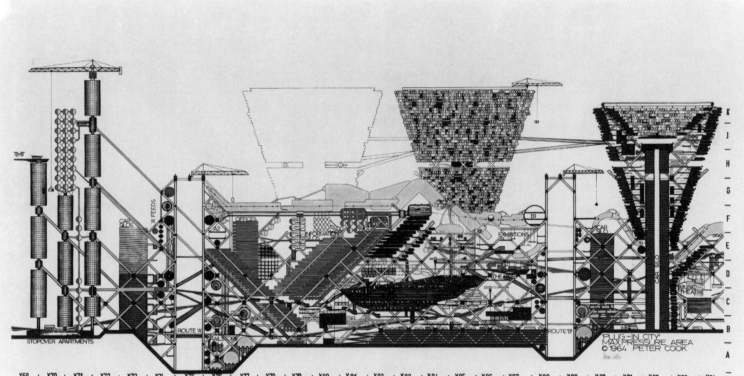

PLUG-IN CITY
MAX PRESSURE AREA
© 1964 PETER COOK

X69 | X70 | X71 | X72 | X73 | X74 | X75 | X76 | X77 | X78 | X79 | X80 | X81 | X82 | X83 | X84 | X85 | X86 | X87 | X88 | X89 | X90 | X91 | X92 | X93 | X94

Cedric Price
City of the Future Project

Perspectives. c. 1965. Crayon, ink, and graphite on paper, 36" × 15'9¾"
(91.6 × 481.9 cm). Gift of The Howard Gilman Foundation, 2000

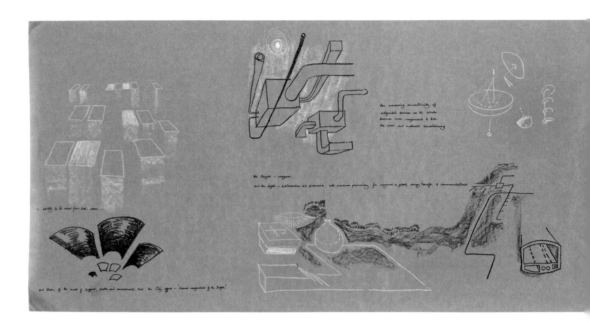

Hans Hollein
Aircraft Carrier City in Landscape Project

Exterior perspective. 1964. Cut-and-pasted printed paper on gelatin silver photographs mounted on board, 8½ × 39⅜" (21.6 × 100 cm). Philip Johnson Fund, 1967

When Hans Hollein announced that "everything is architecture," he could have been not only expressing his view of architecture's all-encompassing nature but making an autobiographical statement: his accomplished career as an architect has run alongside his work as an artist, planner, teacher, and writer, and all of these activities have mutually influenced each other. His designs reflect this diversity, ranging over the last three decades from small shops, exhibition installations, and furniture to museums, civic buildings, urban planning, and environmental projects.

All of Hollein's drawings in this book are from his Transformations series, created between 1963 and 1968. In each, an agricultural or

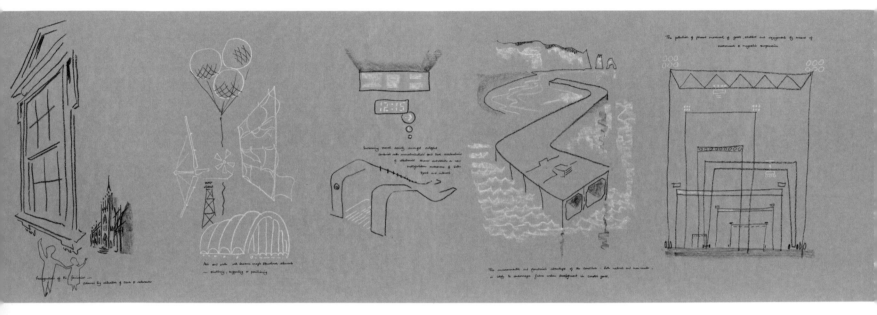

Architectural drawings have a variety of uses: to instruct, inform, indulge, confuse, confirm, congratulate, and console.

— Cedric Price

Cedric Price belonged to a 1950s generation of British architects and educators who were intensely concerned with an architecture of the future. At the same time, they saw architecture as the ultimate *social* art. Price's personal vision of the city, then, was inventive and current while also expressing his sense of architecture's moral obligations: fascinated by new technology, he also believed that its use must be appropriate, playing a role in society that would serve the public and further human freedom and

flexibility rather than confining them. His ideas were visionary but were grounded in the realization that architecture must work for all people.

This drawing for a City of the Future comprises fourteen vignettelike perspectives, with accompanying texts, that together can be considered a summary of ideas about the city that Price had presented in more detail in earlier projects. One of his principles was that the elements that make up the city—buildings, service devices—must respond to the user automatically. Essentially he was calling for a form of artificial intelligence, an idea he had developed in his Pottery Thinkbelt Project of 1963, an unconventional higher-education facility that, if built, would have been located in a depressed industrial area. He also

refuted the ancient assumption that buildings are stationary, suggesting instead that buildings of the modern age could move. The traveling gantry crane and suspended rooms and walkways that he had worked out in his Fun Palace Project of 1960–61 reappear in more general terms in the City of the Future through the description, "the potential of phased movement of goods, shelters and equipment by means of mechanical and magnetic suspension."

—Matilda McQuaid

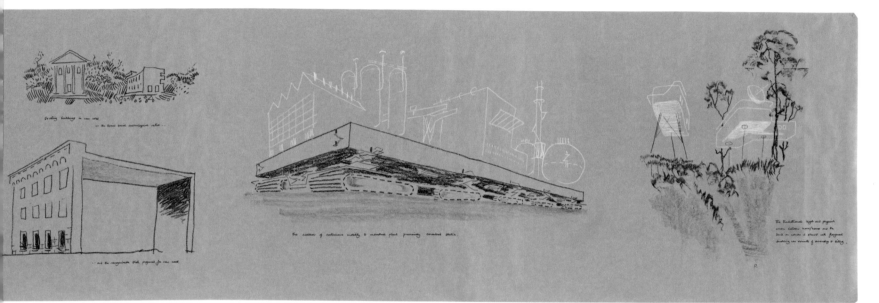

Existing buildings in new role
... on the formal street arrangement within...

... and the reorganised plots proposed for new work.

The addition of continuous mobility to industrial plant previously considered static.

The traditional light and fragrant areas between work/home are to land on which is placed not fragment dividing into smaller granularity of living.

urban landscape, often apparently barren, becomes the site for a monumental object. The drawings are visual parodies of Le Corbusier's concept of architecture as an object in the landscape, an idea exemplified in his seminal book *Vers une architecture* (Toward a new architecture), with its images of ocean liners, automobiles, and airplanes—examples of technological ingenuity that stand as singular objects, more worthy of an absolute and dominant place in the world than any other current example of monumental architecture.

More important in both Le Corbusier's and Hollein's projects, however, is the reference to the machine. Like his Austrian colleagues Walter Pichler and Raimund Abraham, Hollein proclaimed the essential role of the machine in the world: "Today, for the first time in human history, at this point in time when an immensely advanced science and perfected technology offer us every means possible, we build what and how we will, we make an architecture that is not determined by technology but utilizes technology, a pure, absolute architecture." This fascination with the machine was central to the Museum's thematic exhibition *Architectural Fantasies: Drawings from the Museum's Collection* (1967), which also featured the work of Pichler and Abraham.

Hollein's lack of interest in any architectonic style is exemplified by his appropriation of the forms of the sparkplug, aircraft carrier, and tomb/boxcar (pp. 136–37). In their new contexts these objects become symbolic relics, their old functions transformed into unexpected ones of memorial and renewal. The Aircraft Carrier City in Landscape Project led Hollein on to a group of site photographs he took in 1964, dispensing with buildings altogether and declaring the forms of the land themselves to be architectural statements—another proof that "everything is architecture".

—Matilda McQuaid

Hans Hollein

Highrise Building: Sparkplug Project

Exterior perspective. 1964. Cut-and pasted printed paper on gelatin silver
photograph, 4¾ × 7¼" (12.1 × 18.4 cm). Philip Johnson Fund, 1967

Hans Hollein
Urban Renewal in New York Project, New York City, New York

Aerial perspective. 1964. Cut-and-pasted gelatin silver photograph on gelatin silver photograph, 8⅛ × 10" (20.6 × 25.4 cm). Philip Johnson Fund, 1967

Ron Herron (Archigram)
Walking City on the Ocean Project

Exterior perspective. Project: 1964–66. Drawing: 1966. Cut-and-pasted printed and photographic papers and graphite covered with polymer sheet, 11½ × 17" (29.2 × 43.2 cm). Gift of The Howard Gilman Foundation, 2000

Ron Herron describes himself as an architect who "attempts to make architecture by fusing building, technology, and art to make something 'special' for the user." He was a founding member of Archigram, the British group that generated some of the most influential architectural work of the 1960s and '70s through admixtures of science fiction–like imagery and popular culture. Like his contemporaries in Archigram, and like the Austrians Raimund Abraham, Hans Hollein, and Walter Pichler, Herron produced an architecture rooted in advanced technology. Not surprisingly, the city was one of the most popular subjects of Archigram's creative visions, which made "Living Cities," "Plug-In Cities" and "Walking Cities" exemplary possibilities of this truly organic evolutionary form.

Walking City on the Ocean is one of Herron's many drawings addressing the concept of indeterminacy, or of an architecture that can change. The Walking City comprises a series of giant vehicles, each containing the static elements of the urban aggregate and all collectively making up a metropolis. For Cedric Price, an architect who shares concerns with Archigram, the parts of the Walking City were living creatures that "roam the globe forming and reforming." There is a military quality to their tanklike structural vocabulary, described in Herron's strong graphic language, although no tank would have their skylightlike tension-skinned roofs. In fact the Walking City is not unlike some of the engineering accomplishments seen at Cape Kennedy—mobile structures that traverse the landscape.

—Matilda McQuaid

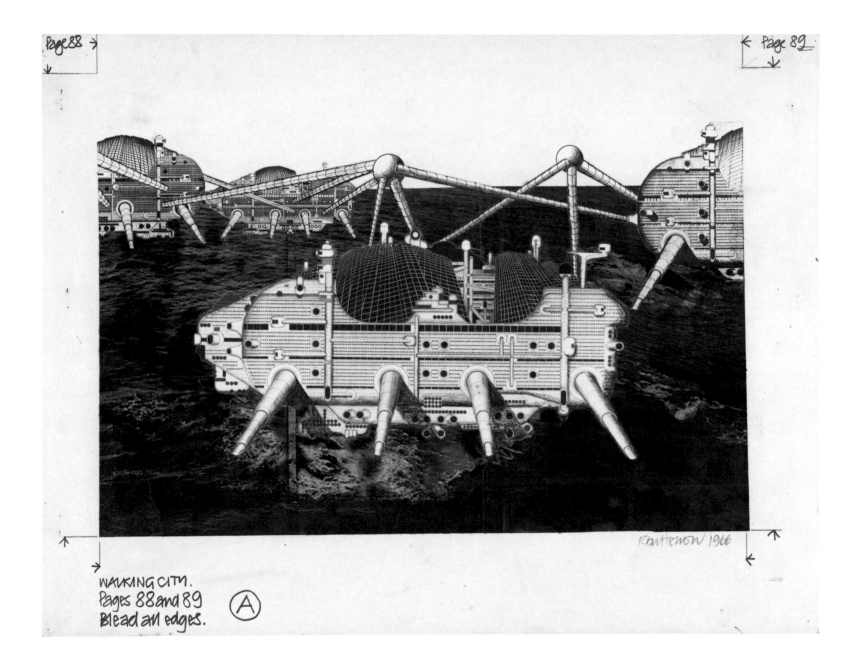

Rontenow 1966

WALKING CITY.
Pages 88 and 89
Bleed all edges.   (A)

R. Buckminster Fuller and Shoji Sadao

Tetrahedron City Project, Yomiuriland, Japan

Aerial perspective. c. 1968. Cut-and-pasted gelatin silver photograph on gelatin silver photograph with airbrush, 11 × 14" (27.9 × 35.6 cm). Gift of the architects, 1974

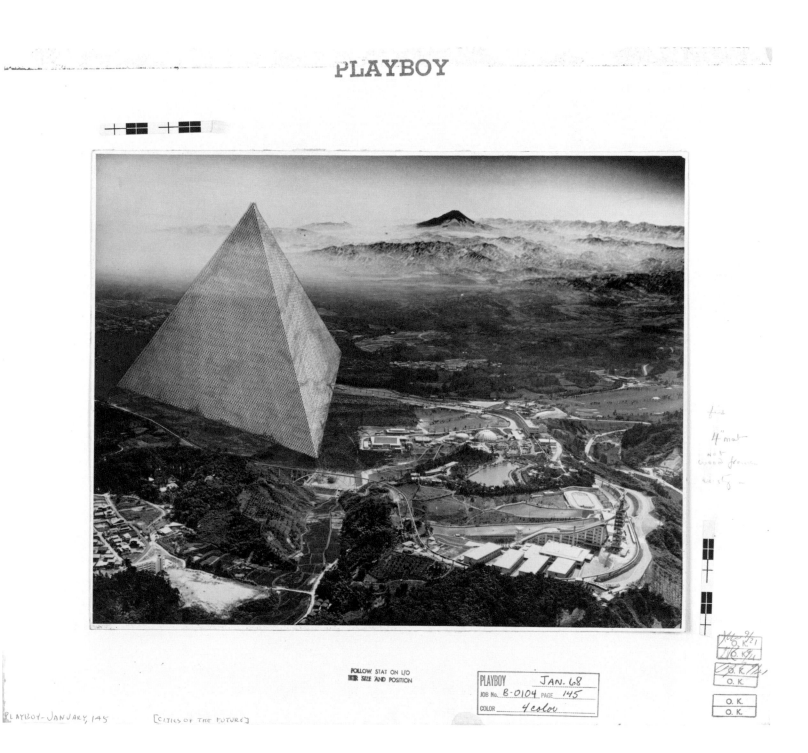

FOLLOW STAT ON L/O
HER SIZE AND POSITION

PLAYBOY   JAN. 68
JOB No. B-0104 PAGE 145
COLOR ___ 4 color

PLAYBOY- JANUARY, 145   [CITIES OF THE FUTURE]

Friedrich St. Florian
New York Birdcage–Imaginary Architecture Project, New York City, New York

Perspective from above and plan. 1968. Color pencil on architectural photo reproduction, 33½ × 35⅛" (85.1 × 89.2 cm). Philip Johnson Fund, 1974

The visionary architect Friedrich St. Florian has explored the idea of alleviating urban problems not by building taller buildings and larger cities but by creating spaces that are only present when activated–a Manhattan office building, for example, that is only there when in use, from nine to five on weekdays. In this vein the New York Birdcage–Imaginary Architecture Project describes the non-physical "waiting rooms" charted by the airplanes that circulate in holding patterns above the greater New York area. This drawing illustrates their paths, the different colors indicating different "rooms." As in solid, earthbound architecture, each room is a dimensional space, with a floor, a ceiling, and walls, but it has no physical structure; existing only when "drawn" by the moving airplane, it depends entirely upon the airplane's presence and on the pilot's and air-traffic controller's consciousness of designated coordinates. Once the craft has moved on, the parameters become

irrelevant and the room disappears. St. Florian sees these "transparent, elusive, magnificent" areas as imaginary forms suspended over our cities.

Although St. Florian is known for his design of the National World War II Memorial, scheduled to be completed on the Mall in Washington, D.C., in 2003, he has spoken of the "nuisance" of projects "actually being built." As if working on paper shared in that nuisance, the Birdcage drawing itself exemplifies transience: it is drawn on a photographic reproduction of a map of New York, a base or template on which the imaginary architecture's temporary waiting rooms are overlaid in the light, relatively impermanent medium of colored pencil.

—Bevin Cline

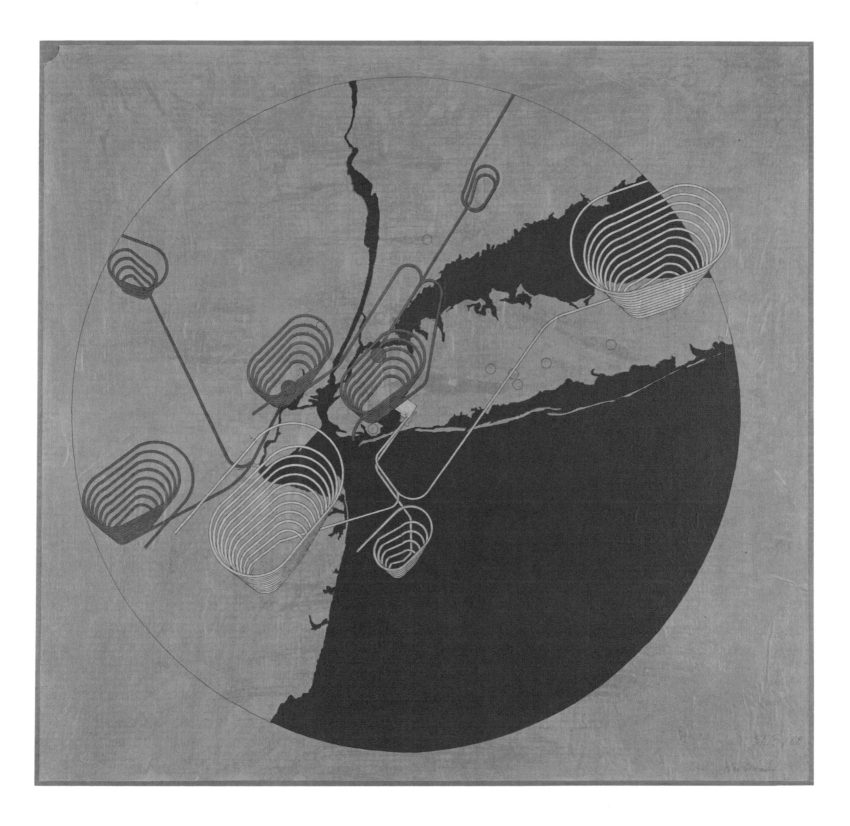

Superstudio (Cristiano Toraldo di Francia, Gian Piero Frassinelli, Alessandro Magris, Roberto Magris, Adolfo Natalini)
The Continuous Monument Project, New York Extrusion, New York City, New York
Aerial perspective. 1969. Graphite, color pencil, and cut-and-pasted printed paper on cardboard, 38 × 25¾" (96.5 × 65.4 cm). Drawing attributed to Adolfo Natalini. Gift of The Howard Gilman Foundation, 2000

In the context of utopian European architecture of the late 1960s and '70s, Superstudio was the most poetic and incisive group to come out of Italy. Founded in Florence in 1966 by Cristiano Toraldo di Francia and Adolfo Natalini, who were then joined by Gian Piero Frassinelli, Alessandro Magris, Roberto Magris, and later Alessandro Poli, the group contributed powerful visions to the international movement that was attempting to design the ideal city of the future. Clearly inspired by the style of the British Pop art movement and the Independent Group, Superstudio displayed remarkable rendering skills in their stunning drawings and photomontages.

This image depicts a Manhattan "by the yard," a monumental extrusion of the cityscape's profile. In Natalini's words, the Continuous Monument is "a single piece of architecture to be extended over the whole world. [Its] static perfection moves the world through the love that it creates, [through] serenity and calm, [and through its]

sweet tyranny." The members of Superstudio, like many of their architect contemporaries, were searching for a new paradigm for the city. They had an optimistic take on urban sprawl, which today is viewed as simultaneously inevitable, unsustainable, and largely negative but at the time seemed part of a global movement toward urbanization that appeared to many as a glorious model for the future. Quoting Karl Marx, the father figure of communism, and Guy Debord, the theoretician of the society of the spectacle, Superstudio were at once esoteric, youthful, and exuberant. Lying on the border of science fiction, their work was a quintessential product of the imagination and ideology of the period, and still surprises and inspires radical architects today.

—Paola Antonelli

From: THE MANHATTAN TRANSCRIPT # New York. EXTENSIONS. Bernard Tschumi 1969

Andrea Branzi
Residential Park, No-Stop City Project

Plan. 1969. Ink, cut-and-pasted self-adhesive polymer sheet and pressure-transferred printed film on tracing paper taped to paper, 39¼ × 27⅜" (99.7 × 69.5 cm). Gift of The Howard Gilman Foundation, 2000

Andrea Branzi, Gilberto Corretti, Paolo Deganello, and Massimo Morozzi founded the Italian avant-garde group Archizoom in 1966. They were inspired by the architectural group Archigram, and by its technological projects for urban utopias; in fact they took their name in part from the name of the British group and in part from the title—Zoom—of an issue of its publication, Archigram. Archizoom was a key participant in the "radical architecture" movement of the 1960s, which reacted against modernist architecture and downplayed practical concerns in favor of a more imaginative, science-fiction-like approach.

The principle behind the No-Stop City was the idea that advanced technology could eliminate the need for a centralized modern city. The group members wrote, "The factory and the supermarket become the specimen models of the future city: optimal urban structures, potentially limitless, where human functions are arranged spontaneously in a free field, made uniform by a system of micro-acclimatization and optimal circulation of information." The drawings and photomontages that constitute the project were intended to demonstrate these ideas rather than to serve as the plan for an actual city. This plan, drawn by Branzi, illustrates a fragment of a metropolis that can extend infinitely through the addition of homogenous elements adapted to a variety of uses. Free-form organic shapes—representing park areas—and residential units are placed haphazardly over a grid structure, allowing for a large degree of freedom within a regulated system. Like a replicating microorganism, the city seems to subdivide and spread, lacking center or periphery.

—Melanie Domino

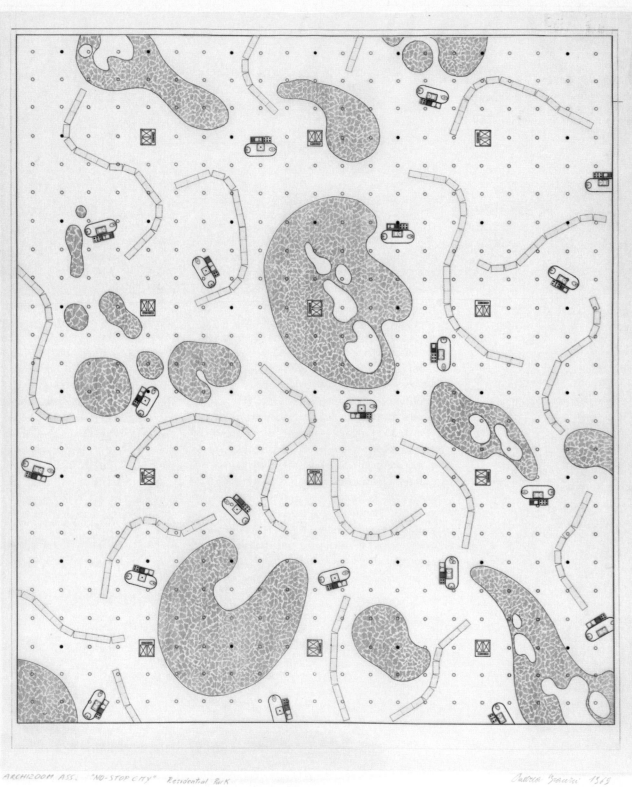

ARCHIZOOM ASS. "NO-STOP CITY" Residential Park   Andrea Branzi 1969

Aldo Rossi

Cemetery of San Cataldo, Modena, Italy

Aerial perspective. Project: 1971–84. Drawing: 1971. Crayon and graphite on sepia diazoprint, 24 × 49¾" (61 × 126.4 cm). Gift of The Howard Gilman Foundation, 2000

Aldo Rossi designed the Cemetery of San Cataldo for a 1971 competition that called for an extension to the existing nineteenth-century Costa Cemetery. Employing conventions of perspective developed in the fifteenth century, Rossi uses an aerial view to give a sense of the cemetery in both plan and elevation. One enters this wall-enclosed space through a gate opposite what seems to be an abandoned house, a cubic structure designed as a collective or nondenominational temple to be used for funeral, religious, or civil ceremonies. As one proceeds along the central axis, it passes through successive rectangular structures, riblike ossuaries that rise in height as they diminish in length. The journey is punctuated by a cone-shaped smokestack monumentalizing a communal grave for the unknown, and referencing the industrial landscape beyond. Rossi's design is rooted in an Enlightenment typology of the cemetery as a walled structure set on the outskirts of town. It not only recalls the adjacent Costa Cemetery but, as Rossi says, "complies with the image of a cemetery that everyone has." A structure without a roof, it is a deserted building intended for those who no longer need the protection of shelter—a house for the dead in which life and death exist as a continuum within the collective memory.

Through his use of aerial perspective, elemental form, and color, Rossi constructs a visual passage through the drawing that corresponds to the journey *contra natura* through the cemetery. Shadows stem from a particular light source yet reference no particular time of day. Perspective, traditionally universalizing, is colored with a Northern Italian palette, and draws our eye not back into space but rather up the page. Like the cemetery itself, the drawing presents a road toward abandonment in which time seems to stand still.

—Tina di Carlo

Superstudio (Cristiano Toraldo di Francia, Gian Piero Frassinelli, Alessandro Magris, Roberto Magris, Adolfo Natalini)

The First City, from the Twelve Ideal Cities Project

Aerial perspective. 1971. Photolithograph, 27¾ × 39⁵⁄₁₆" (70.2 × 100.6 cm). Given anonymously

Gaetano Pesce
Housing Unit for Two People Project

Axonometric section. 1971. Gouache, watercolor, and graphite with scoring on paper, 39¼ × 26¾" (99.7 × 67.9 cm). Gift of The Howard Gilman Foundation, 2000

Ettore Sottsass

The Planet as Festival Project: Study for Temple for Erotic Dances

Aerial perspective and plan. Project: 1972–73. Drawing: c. 1972–73. Graphite and cut-and-pasted gelatin silver photograph on paper, 13 $\frac{15}{16}$ × 12 $\frac{5}{8}$" (35.5 × 32 cm). Gift of The Howard Gilman Foundation, 2000

Concerned by the deterioration of modern-day urban life, Ettore Sottsass created a futuristic vision of "The Planet as Festival," a place in which goods are free, abundantly mass-produced, and distributed around the globe. Cities, jobs, and money worries are obsolete. Liberated from the demands of bank, supermarket, and subway, people can "come to know, by means of their bodies, their psyche, and their sex, that they are living." To advance this awakening of consciousness, technology moves into the role of heightening self-awareness. Life is in harmony with nature.

The fourteen "Planet as Festival" drawings in the collection, all black and white studies for hand-colored lithographs, depict "superinstruments" designed for our entertainment: a monolithic dispenser of incense, drugs, and laughing gas, set in a campground; rafts for listening to chamber music while floating on a river; a stadium in which to watch the stars and the rising and setting of the sun. This drawing shows a temple for erotic dances, a place in which to learn about sexuality. The humorous, cartoonlike perspective of the temple is juxtaposed with a traditional floor plan reminiscent of ancient Egyptian religious complexes. Phallic and orificial in form, the temple buildings have the dimensions of architecture but resemble utilitarian design objects—a laboratory beaker, salt and pepper shakers, and more. Sottsass was a founding member of Memphis (1981–88), a design group dedicated to the creation of brightly colored, eccentrically shaped objects devised without reference to functionalist aesthetics, and his background in industrial design is evident in these forms.

—Bevin Cline

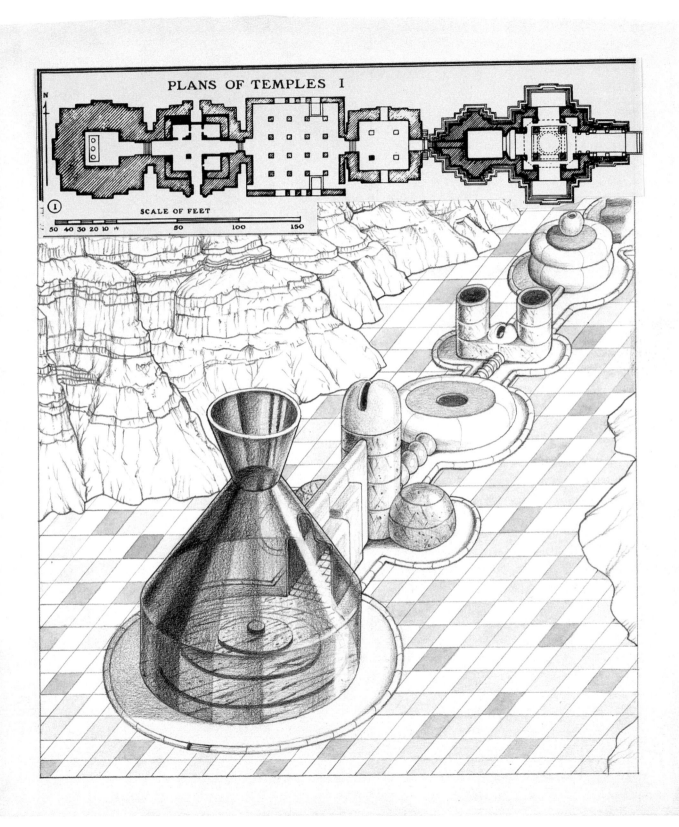

PLANS OF TEMPLES I

SCALE OF FEET

50 40 30 20 10   50   100   150

Rem Koolhaas and Elia Zenghelis with Madelon Vriesendorp and Zoe Zenghelis

Exodus, or the Voluntary Prisoners of Architecture
Project: Exhausted Fugitives Led to Reception

1972. Cut-and-pasted gelatin silver photographs and photolithographs with ink, crayon, and felt-tipped pen on paper, 16 × 11½" (40.6 × 29.2 cm). Patricia Phelps de Cisneros Purchase Fund, Takeo Obayashi Purchase Fund, and Susan de Menil Purchase Fund, 1996

Exodus, or the Voluntary Prisoners of Architecture, is a series of eighteen drawings, watercolors, and collages produced by Rem Koolhaas, Madelon Vriesendorp, Elia Zenghelis, and Zoe Zenghelis. Animated by a text that reads as a simultaneously factual and fictional scenario for the contemporary metropolis, this dense pictographic storyboard reflects Koolhaas's earlier stints as a journalist and screenwriter. The project was ultimately the catalyst for Koolhaas's and his collaborators' formation of their collective architectural practice, the Office for Metropolitan Architecture (O.M.A.), in 1975.

The title "Exodus" alludes to Cold War West Berlin, a restricted enclave encircled by a forbidding wall—in effect, a prison on the scale of a metropolis, and one in which people sought refuge voluntarily. This image becomes the stage for a new urban culture invigorated by invention and subversion. In The Strip, a pencil-drawn aerial view of the walled city, with its approach corridors extending through the surrounding urban fabric, is superimposed on a photograph of London. Exhausted Fugitives Led to Reception depicts the verbal narrative's opening scene: a dark wall, tank traps, and trenches mark the threshold of the captive city, with its somewhat ominous thermograms of skyscrapers rising above the wall, while the "exodus" of "voluntary prisoners" marches toward a checkpoint into what Koolhaas describes as "a continuous state of ornamental frenzy and decorative delirium, an overdose of symbols."

The complex intertwining of images in The Allotments gives meaning to Koolhaas's phrase "an overdose of symbols." The peasant figures bent in prayer come from Jean-François Millet's painting The Angelus (1857–59), but are excised from their context and collaged onto a gridded plinth that runs past a bunker of Tinian marble—the rich material often used by the heroic modern architect Mies van der Rohe. In the background, a surveillance tower rises above the barbed-wire-topped wall. Adding to the complexity, Millet's figures appear as the reconstituted source of their hallucinogenic rendition by Salvador Dalí, in his 1933–35 painting Archeological Reminiscence of Millet's Angelus. Indeed, Dalí's surreal projections and his so-called "critical-paranoid method" are running subtexts in the Exodus narrative.

While O.M.A.'s subsequent work has developed its own trajectory, the graphite-and-watercolor Institute of Biological Transactions—showing a place to act out fantasies of hostility—reveals contemporary influences on the young architects: the orderly composition on a foursquare grid with a diagonal axis recalls contemporaneous work not only by Italian rationalist architects of the 1970s, such as Aldo Rossi, but by the British architect James Stirling.

—Terence Riley

Rem Koolhaas and Elia Zenghelis with Madelon Vriesendorp and Zoe Zenghelis

Exodus, or the Voluntary Prisoners of Architecture Project: The Strip

Aerial perspective. 1972. Cut-and-pasted paper and painted paper with ink, pen, and graphite on photolithograph (aerial view of London), 19¾ × 25⅞" (50.2 × 65.7 cm). Patricia Phelps de Cisneros Purchase Fund, Takeo Obayashi Purchase Fund, and Susan de Menil Purchase Fund, 1996

Exodus, or the Voluntary Prisoners of Architecture Project: The Institute of Biological Transactions

Plan oblique. 1972. Graphite and watercolor on paper, 11⅜ × 16½" (28.9 × 41.9 cm). Patricia Phelps de Cisneros Purchase Fund, Takeo Obayashi Purchase Fund, and Susan de Menil Purchase Fund, 1996

Exodus, or the Voluntary Prisoners of Architecture Project: The Allotments

1972. Cut-and-pasted paper, marbleized paper, and photolithographs with ink and watercolor on paper, 11½ × 16½" (29.2 × 41.9 cm). Patricia Phelps de Cisneros Purchase Fund, Takeo Obayashi Purchase Fund, and Susan de Menil Purchase Fund, 1996

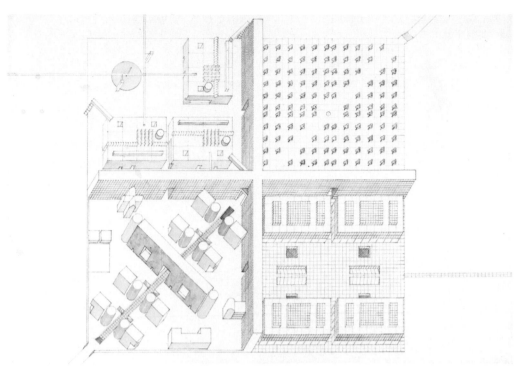

Paul Rudolph
Lower Manhattan Expressway Project, New York City, New York

Perspective to the east. Project: 1967–72. Drawing: 1972. Ink and graphite on paper, 40 × 33½" (101.6 × 85.1 cm). Gift of The Howard Gilman Foundation, 2000

Rem Koolhaas with Zoe Zenghelis

The City of the Captive Globe Project, New York City, New York

Axonometric. 1972. Watercolor and graphite on paper, 12½ × 17⅜" (31.8 × 44.1 cm). Gift of The Howard Gilman Foundation, 2000

Rem Koolhaas with Elia Zenghelis

Roosevelt Island Redevelopment Project, New York City, New York

Axonometric. 1975. Gouache and graphite on board, 29 × 38⅝" (73.7 × 98.1 cm). Gift of The Howard Gilman Foundation, 2000

In honoring Manhattan's "culture of congestion," Rem Koolhaas's 1978 book *Delirious New York* found inspiration where Le Corbusier had seen chaos. Several projects developed by Koolhaas and his colleagues in the Office for Metropolitan Architecture (O.M.A.) appeared in the book; those presented here were also included in the 1978 exhibition *The Sparkling Metropolis*, at the Solomon R. Guggenheim Museum, New York.

The City of the Captive Globe Project, which Koolhaas produced with Zoe Zenghelis, focuses on New York's urban fabric: the relentlessly uniform grid that paradoxically supports a multiplicity of functions and desires. The rendering of each block as a fantastic city-within-a-city creates a virtual catalogue of O.M.A.'s self-proclaimed influences: Salvador Dali's Surreal *Archeological Reminiscence of Millet's Angelus* (1933–35), Le Corbusier's Plan Voisin towers, and El Lissitzky's Lenin Stand all frame the "captured globe," a metaphor for Manhattan's status as an "enormous incubator of the world."

The Roosevelt Island Redevelopment Project, a competition entry prepared by Koolhaas and Elia Zenghelis, offers a more straightforward transformation of the city's architectural typologies. Four identical stepped blocks rise on the waterfront of the East River island. Between them run extensions of the city street grid bordered by low-rise "synthetic brownstones" with stoops, postmodern facades, and mid-block gardens. Seven monumental towers echo the dimensions of the grid.

Koolhaas, German Martinez, and Richard Perlmutter designed the theoretical New Welfare Island Project for just the southern half of Roosevelt Island (once called Welfare Island). At the top of the aerial view, the Queensboro Bridge passes through a convention center, a monumental gateway to Manhattan. Farther south, a "tecton"—a Suprematist device from the work of Kasimir Malevich—hovers over a streamlined Art Deco yacht designed in 1932 by Norman Bel Geddes. At the island's tip the six towers of the New Welfare Hotel rise up opposite a wandering fragment of Manhattan that includes Rockefeller Center and Times Square (including the proposed Sphinx Hotel, designed by Elia and Zoe Zenghelis). The New Welfare Hotel, designed by Koolhaas, Perlmutter, and Derrick Snare, is separately rendered in the third drawing; it is a center for dancing, dining, and general urban pleasure. Overall, Koolhaas writes, the Roosevelt Island project "is intended as a *visual* interpretation *and* resuscitation of some of the themes that made Manhattan's architecture unique; its ability to fuse the popular with the metaphysical, the commercial with the sublime, the refined with the primitive."

—Terence Riley

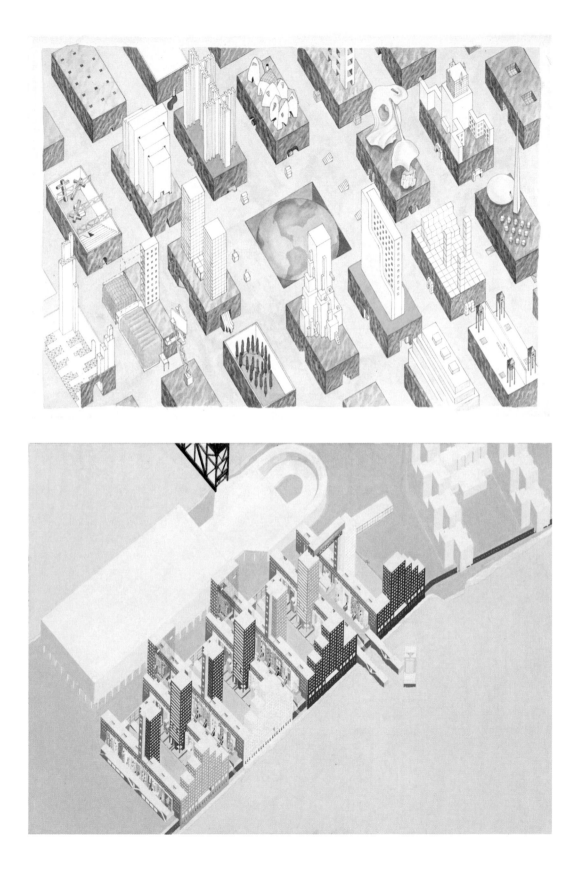

Rem Koolhaas with German
Martinez and Richard Perlmutter

New Welfare Island Project, Roosevelt Island,
New York City, New York

Aerial perspective. Project: 1975–76. Drawing: c. 1975–76. Gouache on
paper, 58 × 40" (147.3 × 101.6 cm). Painting: Zoe Zenghelis. Gift of The
Howard Gilman Foundation, 2000

Rem Koolhaas with Richard
Perlmutter and Derrick Snare

Welfare Palace Hotel Project, Roosevelt Island,
New York City, New York

Cutaway axonometric. 1976. Gouache on paper, 51 × 40½"
(129.7 × 102.8 cm). Painting: Madelon Vriesendorp. Gift of The Howard
Gilman Foundation, 2000

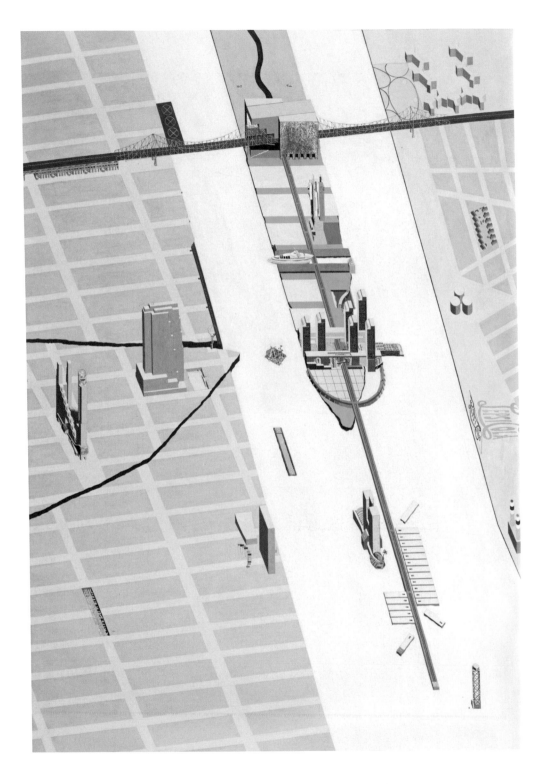

John Hejduk
Wall House 2 (A. E. Bye House) Project, Ridgefield, Connecticut

Combined elevation and plan. Project: 1973–76. Drawing: 1973. Color pencil and graphite on tracing paper on board, 8 × 8⅛" (20.3 × 20.6 cm). A version of this house was built in 2000 in Groningen, The Netherlands. Gift of The Howard Gilman Foundation, 2000

Life has to do with walls; we are continuously going in and out back and forth and through them; a wall is the "quickest," the "thinnest," the thing we're always transgressing, and that is why I see it as the present, the most surface condition.

—John Hejduk

Wall House 2 (A. E. Bye House) is the second in a series of projects that John Hejduk began in the mid-1960s to explore what he called the "first principles" of architecture. Designed for the landscape architect Arthur Edward Bye in 1971, it investigates the wall as the original architectural device. Wall House 2 reinterprets the traditional configuration of a house: instead of being enclosed within one shell, rooms and circulation systems are physically isolated from each other. Kitchen, dining area, bedroom, and living room are stacked curvilinear volumes, linked vertically by an independent circular stair and connected to a study by a corridor. The wall—which Hejduk sets between the rooms and the circulation systems, so that one has to pass through it to move from one room to another—becomes a line of passage,

a boundary. A palette of yellow, green, black, brown, and gray reinforces the division of function, corresponding respectively to the energy of cooking, the nourishment of dining, the dark of night, the earth of life, and a realm of reflection.

The shallow space of Hejduk's drawings has often been called "cubist." In traditional isometric drawing, vertical lines are projected upward from a plan rotated forty or sixty degrees. Such a drawing permits a view of three surfaces: the top and two sides. The lines that Hejduk projects upward, on the other hand, are directly parallel or orthogonal to the plan. The resulting drawing presents two surfaces instead of three, collapsing top and side in a construction that stresses frontality over depth. Combined with the muted palette, this technique moves the drawing toward the role of an intellectual investigation separate from practice, conferring on architecture the power to evoke the mysteries of everyday existence.

—Tina di Carlo

John Hejduk

Wall House 2 (A. E. Bye House) Project, Ridgefield, Connecticut

Isometric. Project: 1973–76. Drawing: 1973. Crayon on sepia diazoprint, 28 × 40⅛" (71 × 102 cm). A version of this house was built in 2000 in Groningen, The Netherlands. Gift of The Howard Gilman Foundation, 2000

Wall House 2 (A. E. Bye House) Project, Ridgefield, Connecticut

Isometric. Project: 1973–76. Drawing: 1973. Crayon on sepia diazoprint, 28 × 40⅛" (71 × 102 cm). Gift of The Howard Gilman Foundation, 2000

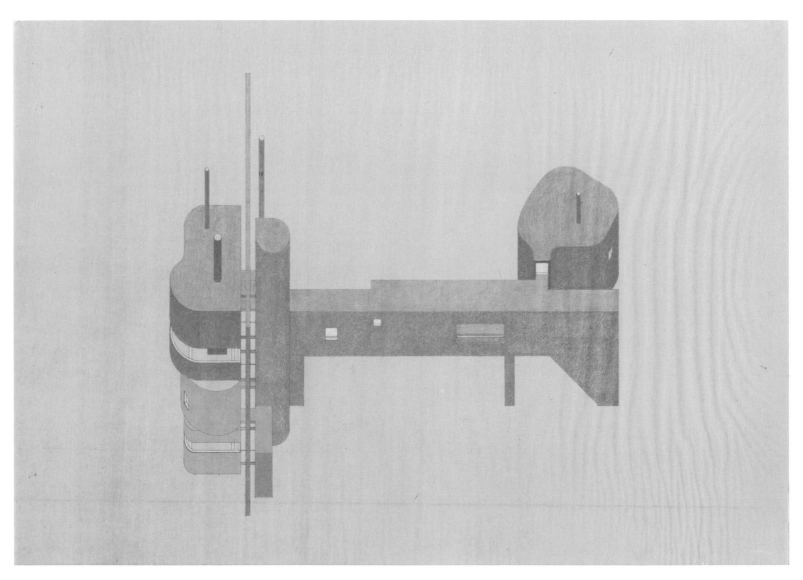

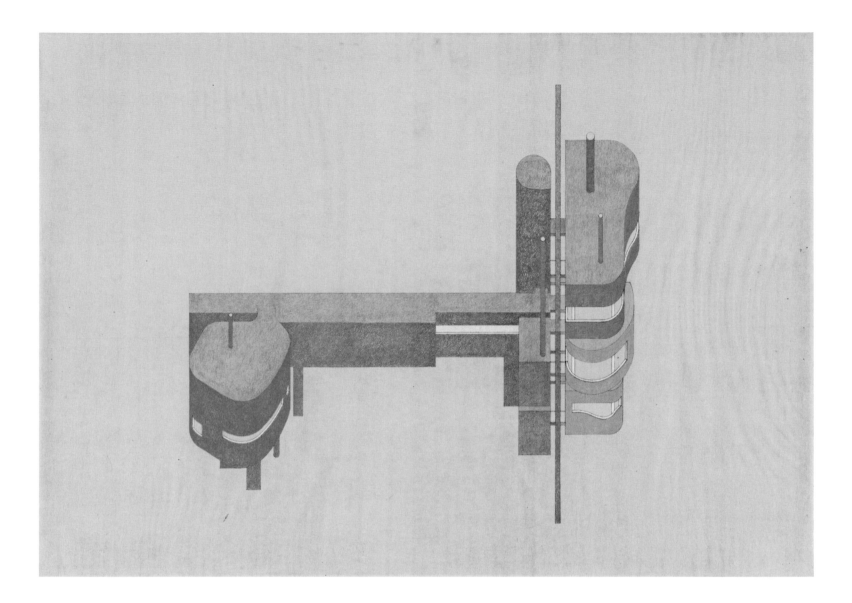

Peter Eisenman
House IV Transformation Study Project, Falls Village, Connecticut

Multiple axonometrics. Project: 1971–73. Drawing: 1975. Ink and color ink on frosted polymer sheet, 13¾ × 44⅝" (34.9 × 103.3 cm). Drawing attributed to Robert Cole. Gift of Philip Johnson, 1980

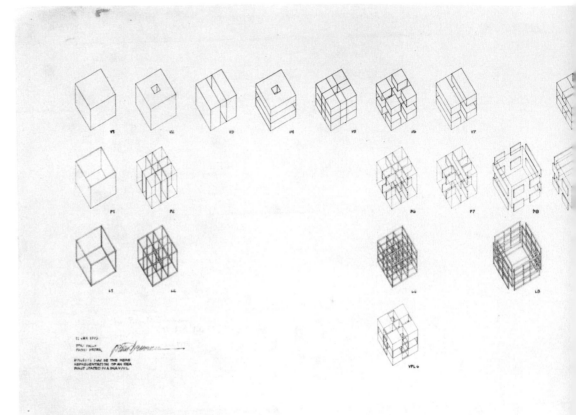

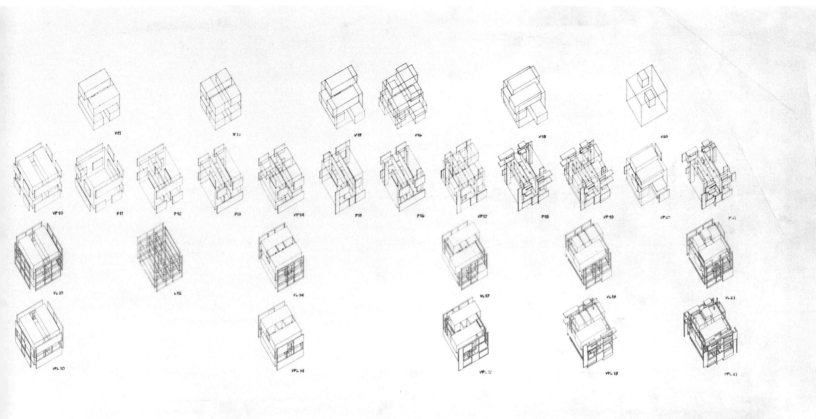

Through a series of eleven houses designed in the late 1960s and 1970s and as the author of numerous texts, Peter Eisenman expounded his theory of an autonomous architecture in which it was no longer necessary for architectural form to result from specific programmatic requirements. Eisenman called these works "cardboard architecture" to describe the way elements such as columns and walls were separated from an "aesthetic and functional context," being used instead as part of a "marking or notational system." To explain the underlying structure of "finite elements" on which his forms were based, Eisenman used the term "deep structure," borrowed from linguistic theory.

The inscription at the lower left of this drawing, "Building may be the mere representation of an idea first stated in a drawing," intimates the importance of drawing in Eisenman's design process. This sequence of axonometrics acts as a diagram, illustrating the transformation of a basic cube into a highly developed spatial configuration. Eisenman has explained, "The diagrams began from a series of rule systems that once set in motion would begin to change the very nature of the rule system itself. The generative rule system would bring about a series of moves, like in a game of chess, in which each move is a response to the last." The original cube was cut, extended, and rotated until the final form of House IV was achieved.

Eisenman first used the concept of the diagram in his Ph.D. thesis in 1963, and it continues to play an important role in his work. Recent projects drawing upon the ideas of philosophers Jacques Derrida and Gilles Deleuze explore the potential of the diagram as an image that is used to create form yet is not in itself a representation of that form.

—Melanie Domino

Massimo Scolari
Urban Passage Project

Isometric. 1974. Watercolor on paper, 7⅛ × 5⅛" (18.1 × 13 cm).
Gift of The Howard Gilman Foundation, 2000

The scholar, painter, and architect Massimo Scolari chose early in life not to build. His small-format drawings, often accompanied by theoretical writings, are not views of an architectural utopia or of a proposed reality; rather, each is intended as a redesign of an architectural form (a fortress, a bridge, a dwelling, a small city, a landscape), "extracting it from its obvious context, redescribing it as though it were being seen for the first time."

In the Urban Passage Project, a remote landscape and an uninhabitable building seem caught in a moment of transformation and construction. An unoccupied cube contains a variety of the familiar architectural elements that would normally constitute a traditional house—masonry cladding, windows, gable roof, cantilevered slabs—yet their scrambled arrangement requires a different interpretation, although a nonspecific one. In his writing, in fact, Scolari has chosen to describe a house through negatives,

a practice he finds revealing and liberating: "The house must not have ribbon windows, must not rest on piloti, must not have a flat roof, must not refer to the tradition of the Modern Movement, must not be solely a living space, must not extend more than two stories above ground, must not rest directly on the ground (must not, therefore, have a base), and must not be symmetrical with respect to its main axis." His one affirmation, meanwhile, reflects an aesthetic requirement in his work, borne out by the delicacy of his watercolor rendering: "Beautiful things are the only friends who never deceive you."

—Matilda McQuaid

Leon Krier
House for Colin Rowe Project

Aerial axonometric. 1975. Ink with gouache on paper, 11 × 8¼"
(27.9 × 21 cm). Gift of The Howard Gilman Foundation, 2000

Leon Krier's House for Colin Rowe is a vignette on the idea of the perfectibility of the classical villa. Cartoonlike, timeless, and without location, it is an architectural fairy tale, yet its delicately drawn double-walled interior and extending ramparts emanate invincibility. This ideal vision of the villa suggests something desirable yet unattainable, and Rowe, a scholar of architecture, has suggested that Krier's work be studied within this utopian context.

Krier, one of the most polemical architects of the 1970s and '80s, has asserted, "I can only make Architecture, because I do not build. I do not build, because I am an Architect." He believes in the perfection of an idea on paper, and his drawing techniques are influenced by the great traditions of Renaissance cartography and by the eighteenth-century architect and printmaker Giambattista Piranesi. Krier exerts a moralistic fervor in denouncing modern architecture and the industrial world, and in promoting a classical language in architecture. He has designed both large-scale cities and small-scale follies, such as this drawing. The clarity of the plan, with its symmetrical arrangement of main facade elements—entrance opening, pediment, and "Palladian" window—recalls sixteenth-century Italian villas by the neoclassical architect Andrea Palladio.

One can interpret Krier's house as a response to Rowe's renowned essay "The Mathematics of the Ideal Villa," published in 1947. Comparing Palladio's Villa Foscari (c. 1550) with Le Corbusier's Villa Stein (1927), Rowe asserts that both architects share a mathematical standard that they impose upon these projects. Krier's bunkerlike villa shares with Palladio and Le Corbusier the essential idea of the cubic block, but is closer in spirit to Palladio's study and reconstruction of Roman domestic architecture.

—Matilda McQuaid

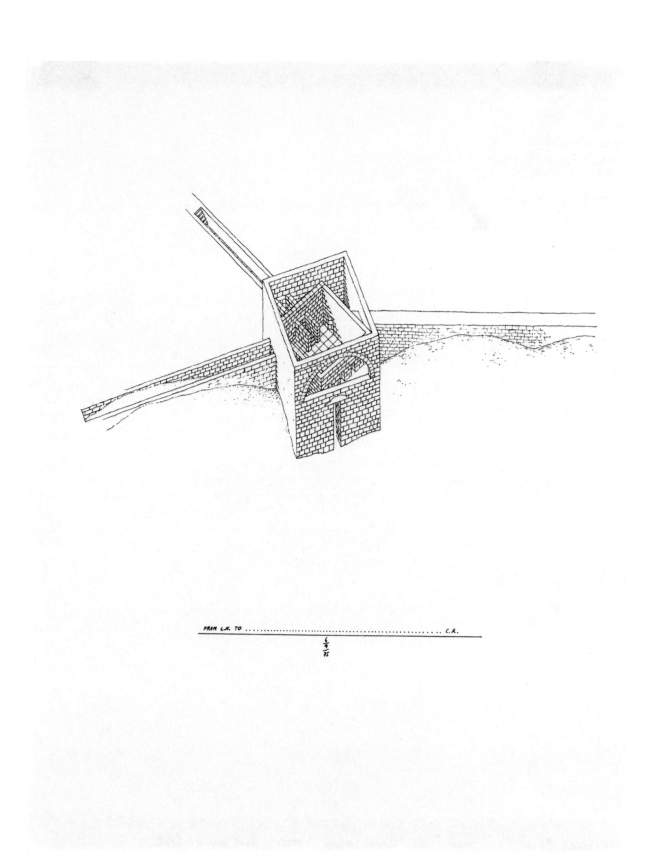

FROM L.K. TO .... C.R.

$$\frac{6}{4}{75}$$

Richard Meier

The Atheneum, New Harmony, Indiana

Plan, preliminary study. Project: 1975–79. Drawing: 1975. Graphite on tracing paper, 16⅝ × 12³⁄₁₆" (42.2 × 31 cm). Gift of the architect, 1984

The Atheneum, New Harmony, Indiana

Elevation. Project: 1975–79. Drawing: 1976. Graphite on tracing paper, 11⅛ × 25¾" (28.3 × 65.4 cm). Gift of the architect, 1984

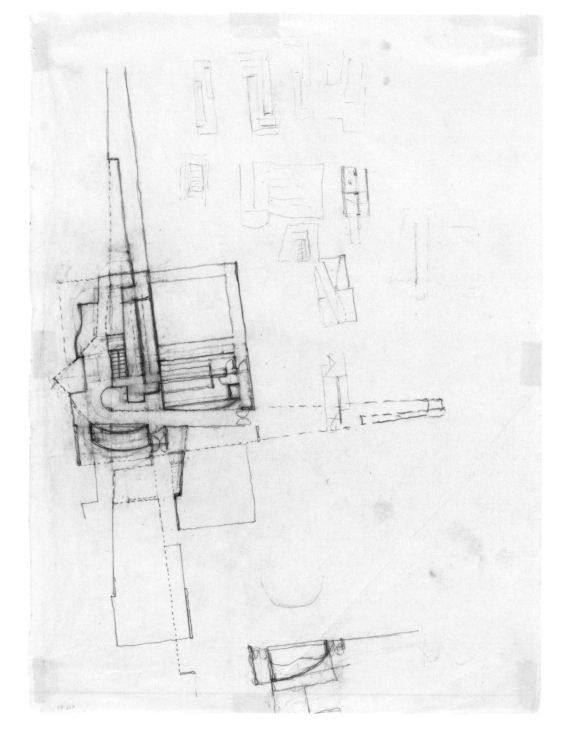

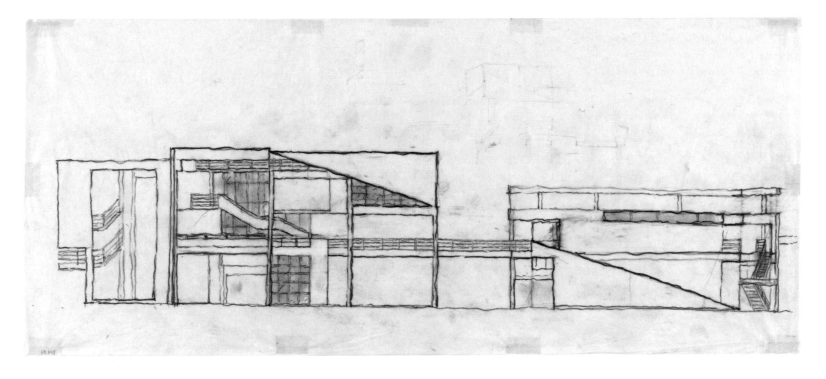

There is nothing superfluous in Richard Meier's lean preliminary studies for the Atheneum, a visitors' center and museum for the town of New Harmony, a utopian community founded in the early nineteenth century. For Meier, drawings are a means to an end. He produces them not for aesthetic purposes—he finds little value in drawing and coloring beautiful facades—but as part of his process of exploring the building's fundamental design, in plan, section, and elevation. Meier's spare graphite line on tracing paper seems fitting to the composition of reductive elements in his all-white building. Yet his economy of line utterly belies the spatial complexity and the drama of light and shadow experienced by the building's visitors.

The historical inspiration underlying much of Meier's work is the early architecture of Le Corbusier, such as the Villa Savoye, an icon of the modern movement. Meier's homage lies in part in his formal vocabulary, with its pilotis, ramps, and pure white forms, but also in his emphasis on the architectural promenade, that is, the journey through the building. Meier has said of the Atheneum that "circulation is the main spatial protagonist of this building and the ramp is its most vital element." This is evident in both of these preliminary studies, which were first exhibited at The Museum of Modern Art in an exhibition devoted to the Atheneum in 1985.

In the plan, the building's principal cross axes can be seen extending beyond it into the landscape, as if connecting metaphorically with the grid of the town to welcome visitors. By rotating one axis slightly off center, Meier creates a dynamic tension that is reinforced by the shifting directions of the path threading through a variety of spaces connected by ramps and stairs. The complexity of these spaces is echoed in the irregular outline of the facade, notably the curved and fluid wall oriented toward the nearby river. The elevation brings the promenade to life by charting its trajectory through the horizontal levels of the building: ramp, stairs, bridges, and balconies activate the overall composition in a careful study of rectangles and grids, planarity and transparency. The drawing conveys a sense of anticipation and excitement, suggesting how this spatially complex building invites exploration and discovery, for the exhibits in the galleries, for the rooftop balcony from which to view the historic town, and for its own intricate sake, as a fitting symbol of the town founders' pioneering spirit.

—Peter Reed

Steven Holl

Gymnasium Bridge Project, New York City, New York

Plan, site plan, and exterior perspective. 1977. Graphite on paper, 22 × 29¾" (55.9 × 75.6 cm). Roblee McCarthy, Jr., Fund, 1989

Steven Holl's Gymnasium Bridge was one of six proposals commissioned by the Wave Hill Center for a bridge between New York's impoverished South Bronx neighborhoods and the parkland of Randall's Island. The project, for four intersecting and overlapping bridges containing usable space as well as acting as passageways, was intended to foster economic development: in Holl's scheme, community members would earn incomes by working on organized recreational activities housed in the bridges—rowing, ice skating, basketball, boxing, and so on—and these activities would in turn attract visitors and custom to the area. Thus the Gymnasium Bridge would not only serve a physical purpose but act as "a vehicle from which destitute persons can reenter society."

This drawing shows three views of the bridge: a plan of the upper level of the main span, a plan of the lower level of all four bridges, and an exterior perspective. The plan of the lower level doubles as a site plan and is continuous with the exterior perspective, while the plan of the upper level is isolated at the top of the drawing. The predominance of the site plan reflects Holl's belief that "architecture and site should have an experiential connection, a metaphysical link, a poetic link." The darkness of the site contrasts with the luminosity of the structure, casting the bridge as a beacon of hope in the community.

This was an early project for Holl. Drawing has always been an important tool in his conception and development of his projects; his renderings, often in watercolor, illustrate his understanding of how the senses perceive architectural spaces. Phenomenology has made appearances in Holl's writings, and as a result of his focus on the human relationship to architecture, his practice is often linked to this philosophical study of reality as it is understood and experienced by the human consciousness.

—Melanie Domino

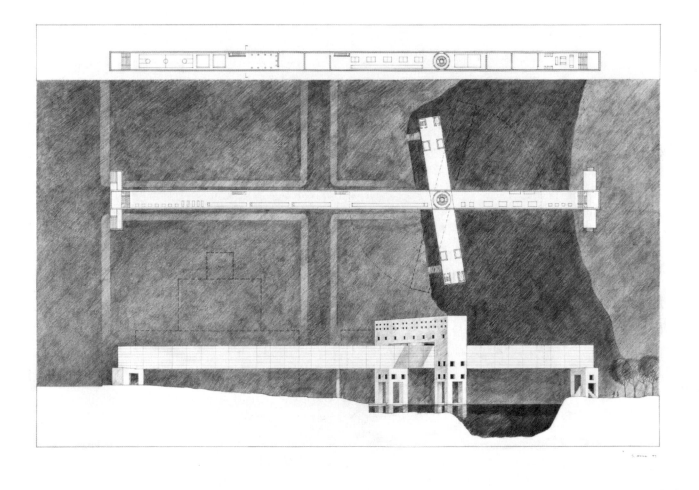

Aldo Rossi
Constructing the City Project

1978. Oil and crayon on canvas, 51³⁄₁₆ × 35⁷⁄₁₆" (130 × 90 cm). Gift of the Architecture and Design Committee in honor of Marshall Cogan, 2001

The city . . . is to be understood here as architecture. By architecture I mean not only the visible image of the city and the sum of its different architecture, but architecture as construction, the construction of the city over time.

—Aldo Rossi

Aldo Rossi's imaginary cityscape is marked by an exploration of what he called the type, the model or norm that gives rise to architecture. Types are prior to and constitutive of forms, which themselves in turn are the ideal geometries into which urban elements are distilled. In this painting Rossi's buildings take the forms of a cube, a cone, a cylinder, and volumes based on the octagon and the rectangle, all forms that recur in his work, and all signifying functions integral to city life. The cube offers a public meeting place, housing political offices and enclosing a plaza; the octagonal tower is a town hall or civic center; the cylinder could be a school, a theater, or a library; and the conical smokestack is an urban monument, the element, for Rossi, through which a city creates its sense of place. Long, fingerlike buildings at ground level contain more public offices, while structures suspended on columns and piers provide housing above and colonnaded walkways below. In the middle ground lie the forms of the single-family house, forms culled from the Italian vernacular—from cabins on Elba, Lombard abbeys, Milanese arcades, industrial landscapes, and other places and scenes.

Influenced by Canaletto's paintings of Venice, Rossi combines a painterly feeling for illusion, and for the space of the imagination, with a passion for structural and spatial types. The metaphysic behind his work, this drawing shows, is architecture as an intellectual construct, but his fantastic elements of pure and rigorous form stir the imagination, evoking a city filtered through memory and constructed over time.

—Tina di Carlo

Gordon Bunshaft (Skidmore, Owings and Merrill)

National Commercial Bank, Jidda, Saudi Arabia

Principal elevation. Project: 1976–83. Drawing: 1977. Felt-tipped pen, color pencil, and chalk on tracing paper, 55½ × 30¼" (141 × 76.8 cm). Drawing: Tom Killian. Gift of Skidmore, Owings and Merrill, 1983

Ricardo Bofill

La Place du Nombre d'Or, Antigone, Montpellier, France

Aerial perspective. Project: La Place du Nombre d'Or plaza, 1978–84; Antigone quarter, 1980–2000. Drawing: c. 1978–84. Ink and felt-tipped pen on tracing paper, 16⅝ × 21⅛" (42.2 × 55.6 cm). Drawing: Jean-Pierre Carniaux. Gift of the architect, 1985

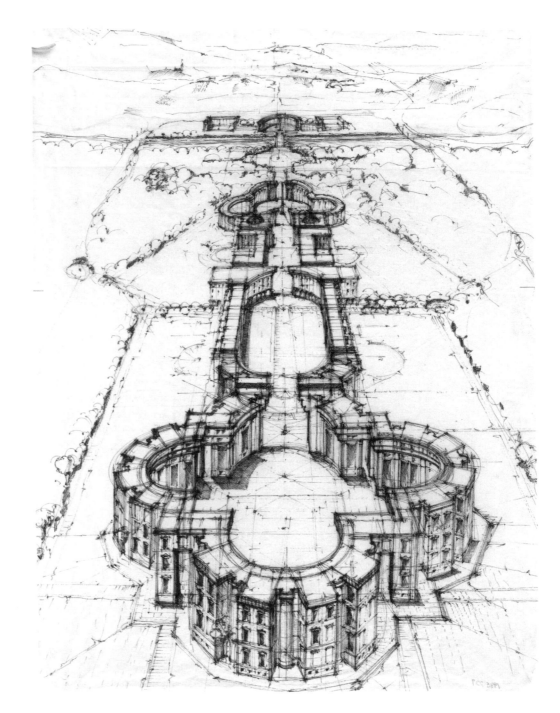

Robert Venturi and John Rauch (Venturi, Rauch and Scott Brown)

House, Northern Delaware

Preliminary study of west elevation. 1978. Felt-tipped pen on tracing paper, 12 × 23½" (30.5 × 59.7 cm). Gift of Venturi, Rauch and Scott Brown, Inc, 1988

Robert Venturi's crucial essays *Complexity and Contradiction in Architecture* (1966) and *Learning from Las Vegas* (1972) served as catalysts in overturning International Style modernism's domination of architectural design. Promoting "messy vitality over obvious unity," in part through the use of such punchy slogans as "Less is a bore," Venturi spoke for an architecture favoring multiple meanings over consolidated form. He also revitalized professional interest in adapting historical styles and devices to contemporary use.

Working with his colleagues John Rauch and Denise Scott Brown, Venturi designed this house for a family of three in northern Delaware, drawing on the vernacular domestic architecture of the region. The design, he has said, is particularly indebted to classic eighteenth-century barns, but these traditional buildings served more as inspiration than as sources to be literally imitated. In this drawing of the western facade, the lunette screen above and the Doric columns below are distorted in proportion and scale. In actuality these bulbous columns are thin, non-load-bearing planes of wood, as flat as the drawing itself. Symbolic rather than structural, they retain their associative power even when stripped of their functional one, and the facade becomes a stage set for the dramatization of domesticity and the local architectural heritage.

—Bevin Cline

Michael Graves

Fargo-Moorhead Cultural Center Bridge Project, Fargo, North Dakota, and Moorhead, Minnesota

South elevation. Project: 1977–79. Drawing: 1978. Graphite and Prismacolor crayon on tracing paper, 11⅞ × 11⅞" (30.2 × 30.2 cm). Lily Auchincloss Fund, 1980

For while it is probably not possible to make a drawing without a conscious intention, the drawing does possess a life of its own, an insistence, a meaning, which is fundamental to its existence.

—Michael Graves

Michael Graves designed the Fargo-Moorhead Cultural Center Bridge as a replacement for a vehicular traffic bridge spanning the Red River and physically connecting the states of Minnesota and North Dakota. On one side of Graves's bridge, in Fargo, lie a concert hall and a public-radio and television station; an interpretive center for the region's cultural heritage lies on the other; and an art museum, shown in this drawing, bridges the two. The drawing is what Graves terms "definitive": preceded by referential and preparatory drawings that are incomplete and fragmentary, it reflects the final proposal for the built object through dimension, proportion, and detail. Graves's palette of terra-cotta and blue visually reinforces the significance of the building as a bridge, an extension of the earth situated midway between sky and water. Inversions of architectural elements do the same: voids in what would traditionally be the sites of keystones, and columns displaced from the sides of arches to their centers, transmit the light above to the water below. In the case of the center column, this vertical connection is literally constructed: the column's capital appears visually as a window of light supported by a shaft of water.

Graves's work, often called "postmodern," is a departure from the functionalist and formal foundations of the International Style. It was significantly influenced by the notion of the architectural sign theorized by Robert Venturi in *Complexity and Contradiction in Architecture* (1966): like Venturi, Graves uses architectural elements representationally rather than structurally or functionally. He is a painter as well as an architect, and his use of drawing alone as a medium through which to design echoes the "pure visibility" of his architecture, in which meaning is collapsed onto the facade in a pastiche of color and form.

—Tina di Carlo

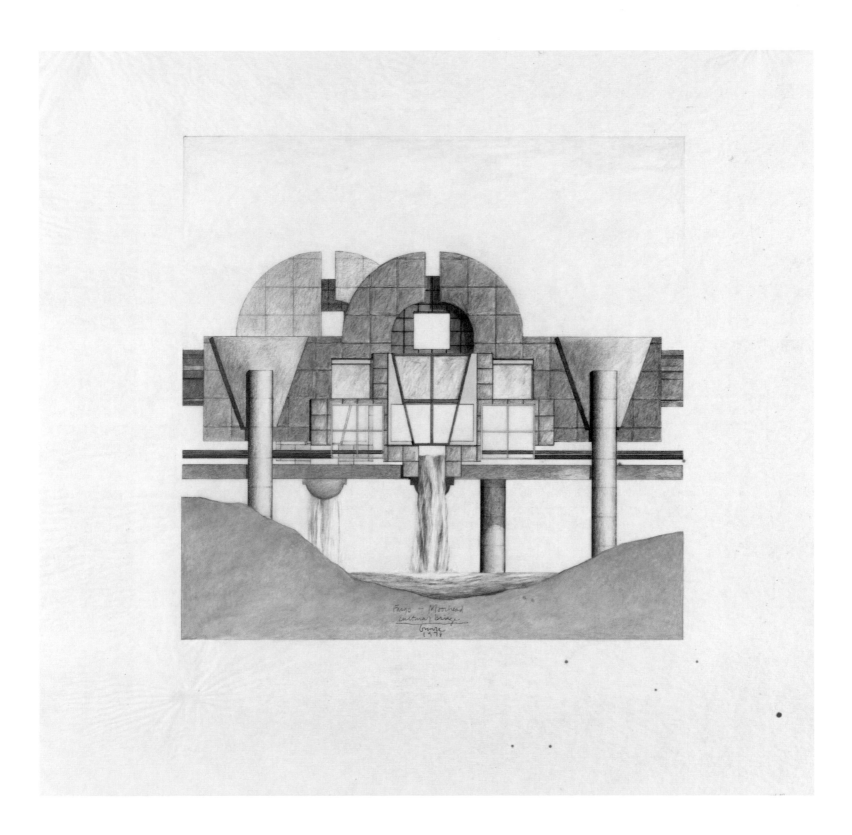

Sir James Frazer Stirling
Staatsgalerie Stuttgart, Stuttgart, Germany

Elevation of gallery entrance and perspective of canopy from below.
Project: 1977–84. Drawing: 1978. Graphite and color pencil on tracing
paper, 21 × 19⅞" (53.3 × 50.5 cm). Gift of the architect, 1982

James Stirling and Michael Wilford &
Associates' postmodern design for the
extension of the Staatsgalerie Stuttgart, a project
also containing a theater and a music school,
won a limited competition in 1977. The architects
were aiming for a building that would be both a
monumental civic structure and an informal one,
reflecting the evolving role of the Western
museum as a place of popular entertainment.
"High tech" in some respects while traditional in
others, the building was intended to relate
simultaneously to its context—the city of Stuttgart,
heavily rebuilt after World War II—and to the
Staatsgalerie's original, neoclassical building, to
which it would be attached.

The design combines a wide range of
architectural references both general and
particular: Romanesque windows (seen in this
drawing), Egyptian entrances, Greek columns,
and allusions to specific buildings such as Karl
Friedrich Schinkel's Altes Museum in Berlin,
Gunnar Asplund's Stockholm Library, and

Raphael's Villa Madama, Rome. These eclectic
juxtapositions of traditional elements, along with
the more contemporary presence of components
in colored metals, result in an inventive and
vibrant modern building.

This drawing is an unusual perspective view
of the main entrance, showing it from various
vantage points at once—both from below and in
elevation. The orange revolving doors and the
blue canopy with its supporting green I-beam are
viewed from beneath, while the wall with its
Romanesque window, and the red beam to
which the canopy is attached, are shown in
elevation. Stirling made the drawing early in the
project, and elements such as the informal and
decorative metallic pink railings were relocated in
the final design.

—Bevin Cline

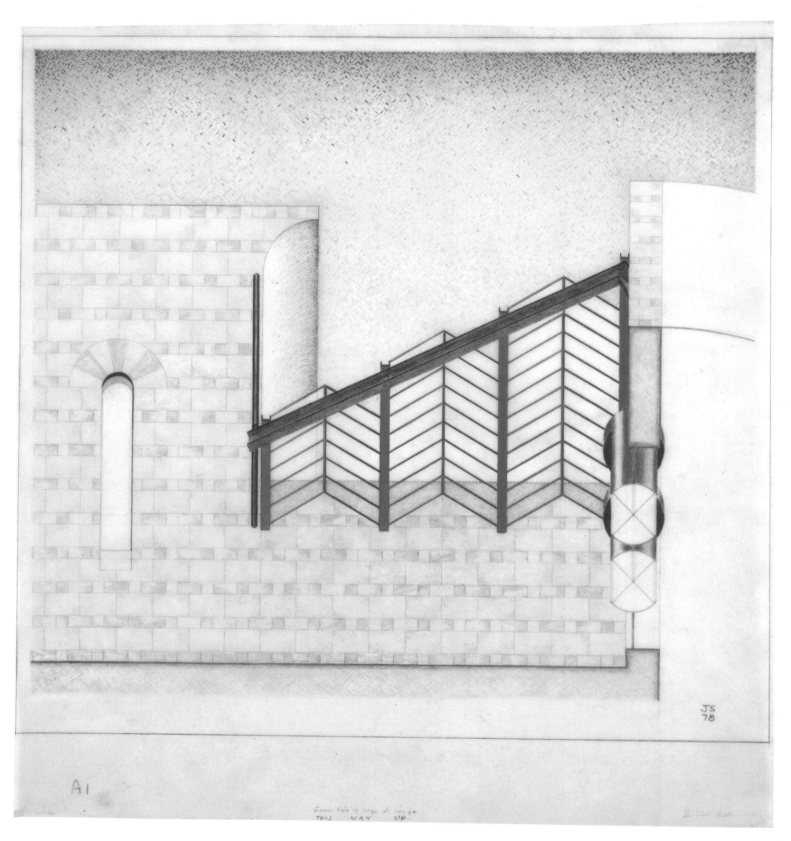

From here to edge of image
THIS WAY UP

A1

JS
78

Emilio Ambasz
Pro Memoria Garden Project, Project for a Labyrinth, Lüdenhausen, Germany

Aerial perspective. 1978. Color pencil, color ink, and graphite on paper, 19⅝ × 58⅝" (49.8 × 149.2 cm). Gift of Pierre Apraxine, 1997

Emilio Ambasz's Pro Memoria Garden was the winning entry in a competition sponsored by the townspeople of Lüdenhausen, in what was then West Germany, for a memorial that would serve to remind future generations of the horrors of war. The project consists of a series of small, irregularly shaped gardens with seven-foot-high hedge walls separated by narrow paths. Children of the town of Lüdenhausen would be assigned one of the plots at birth and would begin to assume responsibility for taking care of it at the age of five. This, it was hoped, would teach them a respect for life. Over time, ideally, the hedges would be removed to make a single large communal garden.

This aerial perspective shows the arrangement of the plots into a labyrinth, a form taken from ancient mythology and adapted by Ambasz to create a space for a contemporary ritual. The flatness and the minimalist style of the drawing allow us to appreciate the labyrinth's shape, while the reference in the background to the landscape and horizon line anchors the garden to the earth. Ambasz generally addresses the mystical and poetic side of architecture in his work, even when he is using modern technology. "It has always been my deep belief," he writes, "that architecture and design are both myth-making acts. . . . The architect's or designer's milieu may change but the task remains the same: to give poetic form to the pragmatic." Ambasz's drawings generally represent the end product of a design process that is developed in his mind rather than on paper.

—Melanie Domino

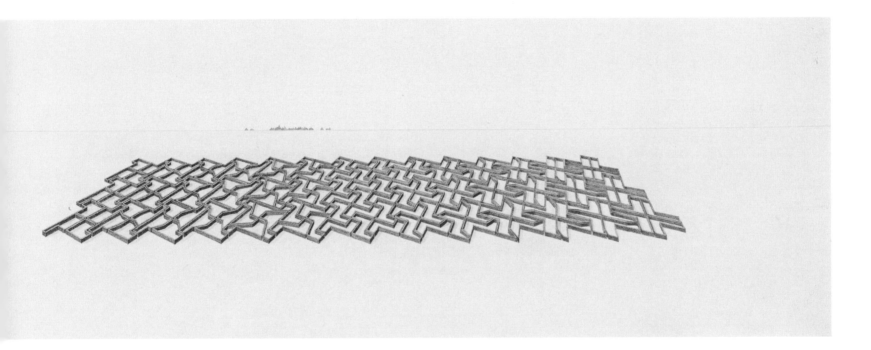

Emilio Ambasz
House of Spiritual Retreat, Córdoba, Spain

Aerial axonometric. Project: 1976–79. Drawing: 1979. Airbrush and graphite on gelatin silver photograph mounted on foamcore, $30\frac{5}{8} \times 25\frac{15}{16}$" (77.8 × 65.9 cm). Gift of the architect in honor of Lily Auchincloss, 1994

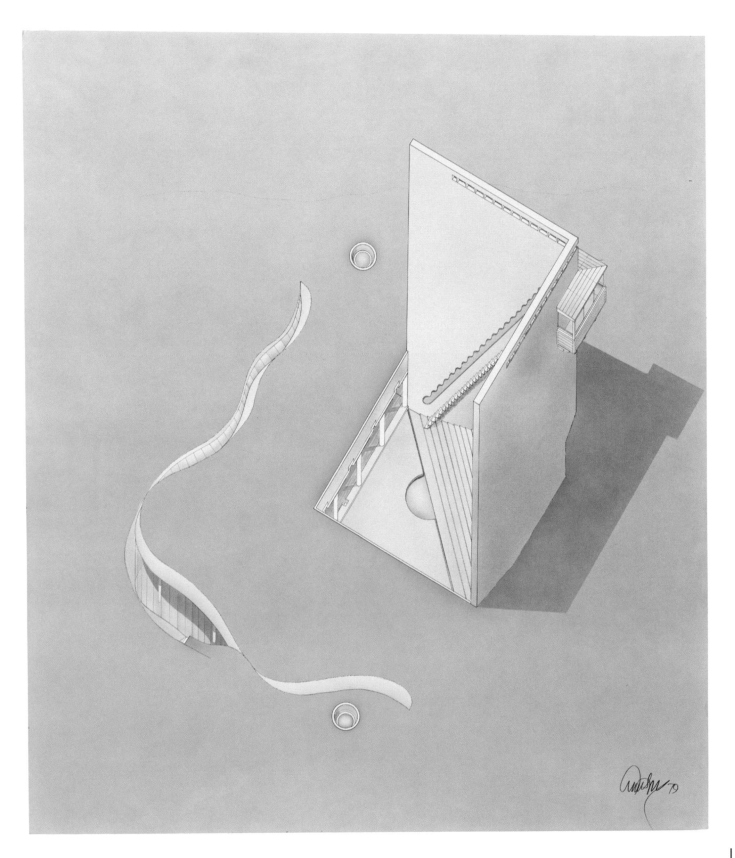

Bernard Tschumi

The Manhattan Transcripts Project, Episode 1: The Park, New York City, New York

Project: 1976–81. Drawing: 1976–77. Gelatin silver photograph, 14 × 18" (35.6 × 45.7 cm). Purchase and partial gift of the architect in honor of Lily Auchincloss, 1995

The Manhattan Transcripts Project, Episode 1: The Park, New York City, New York

Project: 1976–81. Drawing: 1976–77. Gelatin silver photograph, 14 × 18" (35.6 × 45.7 cm). Purchase and partial gift of the architect in honor of Lily Auchincloss, 1995

The tripartite mode of notation [used in The Manhattan Transcripts*] . . . proceeded from a need to question the modes of representation generally used by architects: plans, sections, axonometrics, perspectives. However precise and generative they may have been, each implies a logical reduction of architectural thought to what can be shown. . . . They are caught in a sort of prison-house of architectural language, where "the limits of my language are the limits of my world." Any attempt to go beyond such limits, to offer another reading of architecture, demanded the questioning of these conventions.*

—Bernard Tschumi

Bernard Tschumi's *Manhattan Transcripts* is a theoretical proposition executed through drawing. Drawn between 1976 and 1981 for consecutive exhibitions, its four episodes transcribe imagined events in real New York locales: *Episode 1: The Park* uncovers a murder in Central Park; *Episode 2: The Street (Border Crossing)* chronicles the movement of a person drifting through violent and sexual events on 42nd Street; *Episode 3: The Tower (The Fall)* depicts a vertiginous fall from a Manhattan skyscraper; and *Episode 4: The Block* illustrates five unlikely events occurring in separate courtyards within a city block.

Influenced by the writings of Georges Bataille, Jacques Derrida, and Michel Foucault, and by Guy Debord's notions of *dérive* (urban drifting) and *détournement* (the deflection or rerouting of events and images to subversive effect), Tschumi's *Transcripts* proposes that architecture resides in the superimposition of three disjunctures: space (the fabrication of physical spaces); movement (the movement of bodies in space); and event (program, function, or use). Each of these fields correlates to a graphic device employed, in varying degrees of collapse, in the work's four episodes: architectural-drawing conventions (plans, sections, perspectives, and axonometrics) outline space; a modified form of dance notation diagrams the movement of different protagonists; and photographs direct or witness events. Using film techniques such as the jump cut and the tracking shot to go beyond architectural conventions of representation, Tschumi proposes an architecture of difference and opposition rather than of synthesis and totality. Meaning, no longer fixed, is produced through the subjective sequencing of isolated frames and of disjunctive, multitudinous events.

—Tina di Carlo

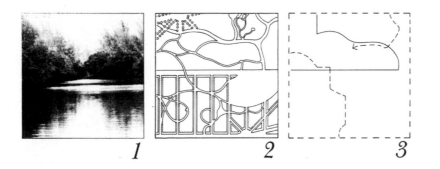

1　　　　　　2　　　　　　3

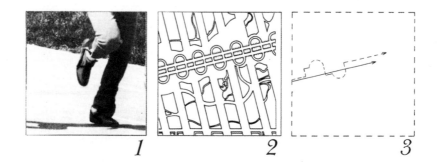

1　　　　　　2　　　　　　3

Bernard Tschumi

**The Manhattan Transcripts Project, Episode 3:
The Tower (The Fall), New York City, New York**

Project: 1976–81. Drawing: 1979. Ink on tracing paper, 48 × 24"
(121.9 × 61 cm). Purchase and partial gift of the architect in honor of
Lily Auchincloss, 1995

**The Manhattan Transcripts Project, Episode 4:
The Block, New York City, New York**

Project: 1976–81. Drawing: 1980–81. Ink and cut-and-pasted gelatin silver
photographs, 19 × 31" (48.3 × 78.7 cm). Purchase and partial gift of the
architect in honor of Lily Auchincloss, 1995

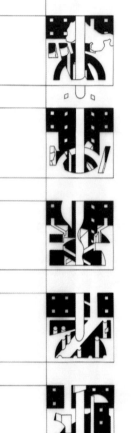

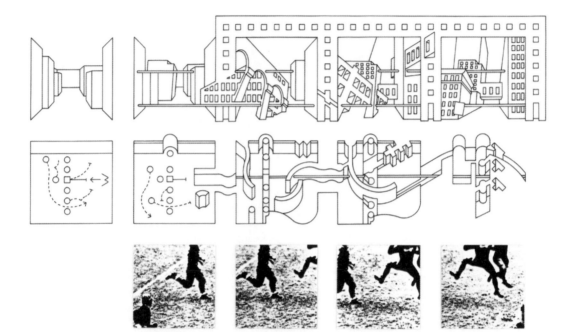

Daniel Libeskind
Micromegas Project: Time Sections

Project: 1978–79. Drawing: 1979. Screenprint on paper, 26 × 36⅛"
(60.6 × 92 cm). Gift of Robert K. and Barbara J. Straus Family
Foundation, Inc., 1999

Daniel Libeskind's Micromegas Project, named after a short story by Voltaire, began with eleven pencil drawings, which subsequently served as studies for a series of twelve prints. Libeskind signed both the prints and the drawings, considering them works of art. Their extraordinary line work was not intended purely as a graphic device but is related to the concept of time: "An architectural drawing," Libeskind writes, "is as much a prospective unfolding of future possibilities as it is a recovery of a particular history to whose intentions it testifies and whose limits it always challenges. In any case a drawing is more than the shadow of an object, more than a pile of lines, more than a resignation to the inertia of convention." In the print shown here, *Time Sections*, projected fragments of architectural elements explode across the surface of the paper, illustrating no single moment of time but alluding to events in

both the past and the future. We look at Libeskind's drawing searching for familiar architectural forms and meanings; instead the lines repel, returning the eye to the surface and ultimately inward to explore the depths of our own imaginations.

Libeskind was once a serious musician—he was a concert violinist by the age of fifteen—and he has done postgraduate work in philosophy and history. This diverse background strongly influenced his thinking as an architect. Libeskind's work is strongly spiritual, and breaks in many respects from architectural tradition. In early projects such as Micromegas, he created drawings that are not representations of a physical space but architecture in themselves.

—Melanie Domino

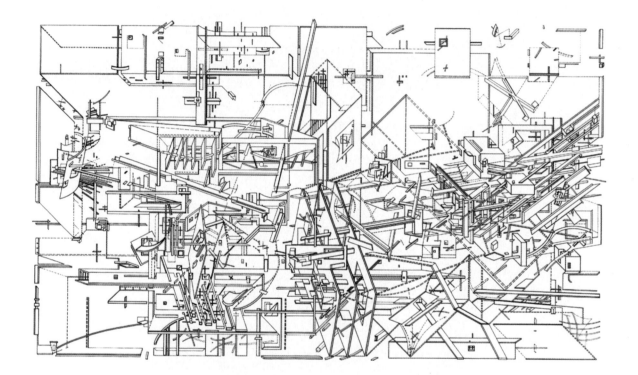

01/90   2: Time Sections   Daniel Libeskind

Coop Himmelblau (Wolf Prix, Helmut Swiczinsky)

Formmutation I Project

1981. Graphite on paper, 11¾ × 16½" (29.8 × 41.9 cm). Frederieke Taylor
Fund, 1988

Zaha Hadid
Parc de la Villette Project, Paris, France

Plan. 1982–83. Ten electrostatic prints on polymer sheets between acrylic sheets with metal screws and supports, 11¾ × 16½" (29.8 × 41.9 cm). Gift of the architect in honor of Philip Johnson, 1996

Parc de la Villette Project: Fields, Paris, France

Plan. 1982–83. Color pencil on tracing paper, 11¾ × 16½" (29.8 × 41.9 cm). Gift of the architect in honor of Philip Johnson, 1996

The drawing is a lens that reveals otherwise imperceptible aspects; it's a method for understanding how things can change and evolve and serve, not for crystallizing a form in a definitive way but to demonstrate the possibilities of what it can become.

—Zaha Hadid

At once a representation of a proposal and an investigation into architecture, Zaha Hadid's drawings for the Parc de la Villette, Paris, present drawing as a way of thinking. These drawings—six from a series of twenty—form a series of overlays that mimic Hadid's conception for the project: stacked planes of uninterrupted space that hover above the landscape. They were produced for a competition sponsored by the French government in 1982, and eventually won by Bernard Tschumi in March 1983, that entailed designing a park for the twenty-first century. The park was to be located in a *terraine vague*, a 125-acre site that had once housed a group of slaughterhouses in the northeast corner of Paris, between the outer fringes of the city and the peripheral highway that borders it to the north. Hadid proposed a series of elevated mobile gardens, which were to move in random or controlled orbits and change with the seasons—a virtual galaxy of kiosks, picnic areas, restaurants, and gardens. One might experience this park the way one sees an architectural section—as a vertical slice through the landscape, where one would encounter unforeseen and infinite juxtapositions of space. Nature in this sense became an artificial construct, and the landscape, rather than a picturesque *paysage*, a laboratory of discovery.

These elements of surprise are the point of both Hadid's project and her drawings. Just as the mechanized movement of the gardens becomes a kind of calligraphy on the ground, Hadid's precise mark-making becomes a form of research into the possibilities of architecture. Her preferred method of black and white drawing explores elemental constructs, and when she does use color, rather than being decorative, it reveals the mood and quality of the space.

Hadid is perhaps best known as a theoretical architect; the Vitra Fire Station, Weil am Rhein, completed in 1993, was her first built work, and the Terminus Nord, a transportation center in Strasbourg, is scheduled to be completed early in 2002. Her affinity with the Russian Constructivists and Suprematists of the 1920s lies less with formal drawing conventions than in an attitude of experimentation without need for conclusion, and in an expression of hope for new forms of architecture that go beyond what we know.

—Tina di Carlo

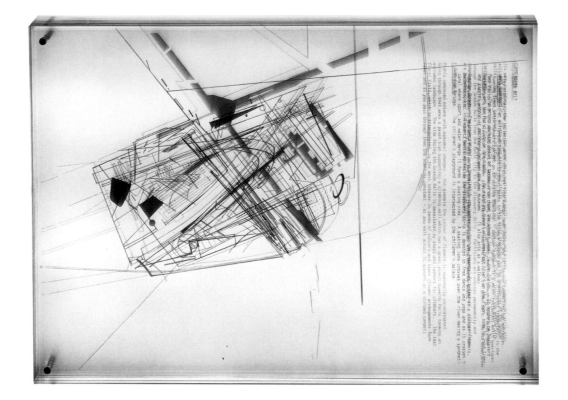

Zaha Hadid

Parc de la Villette Project: Discovery, Paris, France

Plan. 1982–83. Color pencil on tracing paper, 11¾ × 16½" (29.8 × 41.9 cm). Gift of the architect in honor of Philip Johnson, 1996

Parc de la Villette Project: Planetary/Water Strip, Paris, France

Plan. 1982–83. Color pencil on tracing paper, 11¾ × 16½" (29.8 × 41.9 cm). Gift of the architect in honor of Philip Johnson, 1996

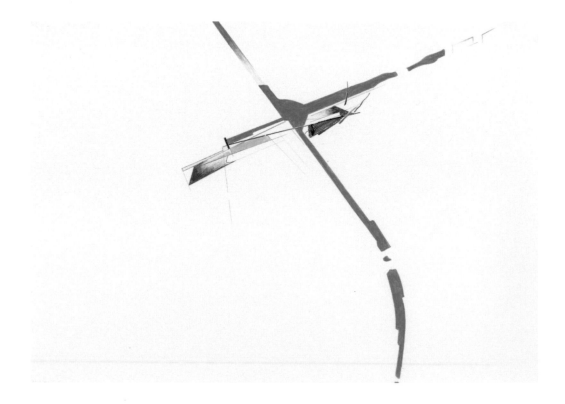

Zaha Hadid

Parc de la Villette Project: Plot Breakdown, Paris, France

Plan. 1982–83. Color pencil on tracing paper, 11¾ × 16½" (29.8 × 41.9 cm). Gift of the architect in honor of Philip Johnson, 1996

Parc de la Villette Project: Base Plan (as Existing) and Moving Elements, Paris, France

Plan. 1982–83. Ink on tracing paper overlay, 11¾ × 16½" (29.8 × 41.9 cm). Gift of the architect in honor of Philip Johnson, 1996

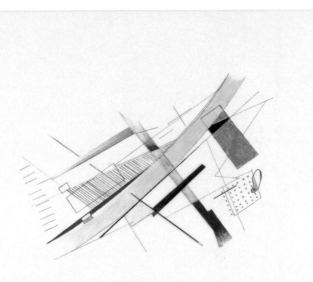

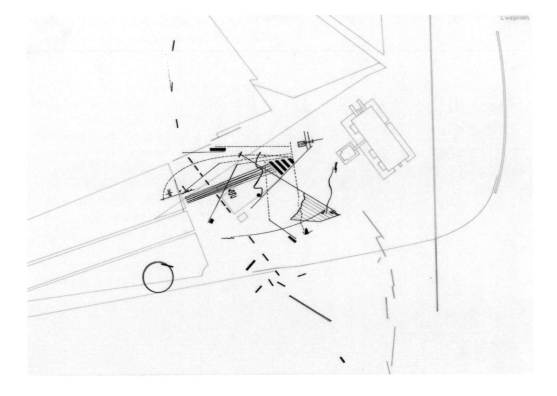

Bernard Tschumi
Follies and Galleries, Parc de la Villette, Paris, France

Frontal axonometrics. Project: 1982–98. Drawing: 1986. Gouache and color ink on gelatin silver photograph, 34 × 50" (86.4 × 127 cm). Purchase, 1992

La Villette had to be built: . . . the finality of each drawing was "building."

—Bernard Tschumi

Bernard Tschumi's drawing of the Follies, one of the three components of his winning proposal in the competition for the Parc de la Villette, Paris, in 1982, seems at first glance limited by the architectural-drawing conventions he eschews in his earlier, theoretical project *The Manhattan Transcripts* (see pp. 204–7). Evenly dispersed as points in a four-by-four grid, each folly (with the exception of that on the lower right) is represented through an axonometric projection, painted red with gouache.

Like *The Manhattan Transcripts*, the design for Parc de la Villette employs three autonomous systems: points, lines, and surfaces. Superimposed over the 125-acre expanse, each system also corresponds to the architectural method of disjuncture that Tschumi applied in the earlier work: points equal events; lines correspond to systems of movement; and surfaces are equivalent to systems of space. The Follies are the points, or pointlike activities, distributed evenly at 120-meter intervals. Each is a permutation of the same basic 10-by-10-cubic-meter frame.

Where Zaha Hadid's proposal for the park (pp. 212–15) can be understood through the simultaneity of a vertical section, Tschumi's tripartite system introduces a cinematic quality, or an order of time and sequence, into the landscape. Meaning is derived through the order of experience rather than the order of structure, as one's experience is conditioned by one's movement. Each Folly becomes an isolated frame within which space, movement, and events are contracted and between which architecture occurs.

Drawn in 1986, four years after Tschumi made his initial proposal, the Follies read here like built objects in the landscape—static, sculptural forms. Yet as one's eye jumps from point to point and passes from medium to medium, the drawing, like the park, is constructed through movement. Red ink and red and white gouache painted over the white line of the photographic image become interchangeable notation systems in which the event forms the backdrop.

—Tina di Carlo

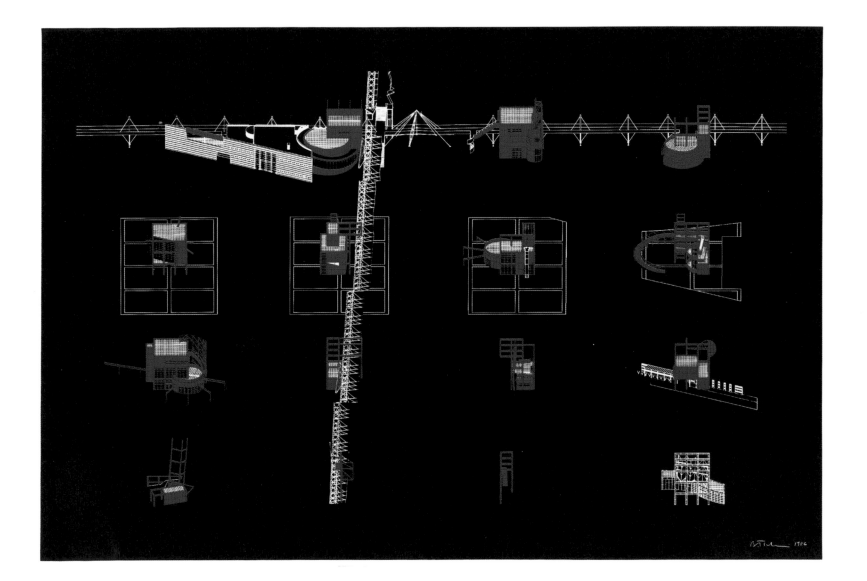

Zaha Hadid

The Peak Project, Kowloon, Hong Kong

Exterior perspective. Project: 1983. Drawing: 1991. Acrylic on paper
mounted on canvas, 51" × 6' (129.5 × 183 cm). David Rockefeller, Jr.
Fund, 1992

James Wines (SITE)
Highrise of Homes Project
Exterior perspective. 1981. Ink and charcoal on paper, 22 × 24"
(55.9 × 61 cm). Best Products Company Inc. Architecture Fund, 1981

James Wines, a founding member in 1970 of the SITE (Sculpture In The Environment) architectural group, described the Highrise of Homes project as a "vertical community" to "accommodate people's conflicting desires to enjoy the cultural advantages of an urban center, without sacrificing the private home identity and garden space associated with suburbia." The plan calls for a steel-and-concrete, eight-to-ten-story, U-shaped building frame erected in a densely populated urban area. The developer would sell lots within this frame, each lot the site for a house and garden in a style chosen by the purchaser. The result would be a distinct villagelike community on each floor, with interior streets. A central mechanical core would serve these homes and gardens, while shops, offices, and other facilities on the ground and middle floors would provide for the residents' needs.

Whereas urban skyscrapers are normally made up of identical, stacked, boxlike units, the Highrise of Homes would allow flexibility and individual choice. The wide variety of house styles, gardens, hedges, and fences described in this intricate rendering provides a sense of the personal identity and human connection that are generally erased by the austere and repetitive elements of architectural formalism. Placing the sociological and psychological needs of the inhabitant over the aesthetic sensibilities of the architect, Wines produces a merge of suburb and city, a collage of architectures collectively created by its inhabitants and by the art of chance. Developers considered Battery Park City, New York, as a possible location for the project, but it was never built.

—Bevin Cline

HIGHRISE OF HOMES

1981 SITE ●●●● JII

Paul Rudolph

Beach Road II Office Tower Project, Singapore

Exterior perspective. Project: 1981–93. Drawing: 1981. Ink and graphite on tracing paper, 79½ × 39½" (201.9 × 100.3 cm). The tower was never built in this form; a revised version of it was, however, named The Concourse. Gift of the architect in honor of Philip Johnson, 1996

Raimund Abraham
Times Square Tower Project, New York City, New York

Exterior perspective. 1984. Graphite and color pencil on cut-and-pasted papers on sepia diazoprint, 33½ × 25½" (85.1 × 64.8 cm). Gift of the architect in honor of Lily Auchincloss, 1994

Sir Norman Foster

Hongkong and Shanghai Bank, Hong Kong

Axonometric and elevation. Project: 1979–86. Drawing: 1985. Ink and color ink on tracing paper, 16½ × 11⅝" (41.9 × 29.5 cm). Gift of the architect in honor of Philip Johnson, 1996

Hongkong and Shanghai Bank, Hong Kong

Elevation and exterior perspective. Project: 1979–86. Drawing: 1985. Ink and color ink on tracing paper, 16½ × 11⅝" (41.9 × 29.5 cm). Gift of the architect in honor of Philip Johnson, 1996

These sketches for one of Sir Norman Foster's best-known buildings are only two of the 120,000 or so drawings that were produced for the project, yet their subjective assertiveness makes them a clear declaration of the architect's technical and visual intentions. Provisional as they appear, they plainly demonstrate the character and stance of the future headquarters of the Hongkong and Shanghai Bank. Made of eight vertical mast assemblies and five great trusses that provide lateral stiffness and support the floors, the complex structure, engineered by the premier firm of Ove Arup & Partners, reveals itself on its surface to dramatic expressive effect. The lateral view, on the right in the drawing on the opposite page, shows the towers that contain the elevators, utilities, and stairs, as well as the trusses working as wind braces.

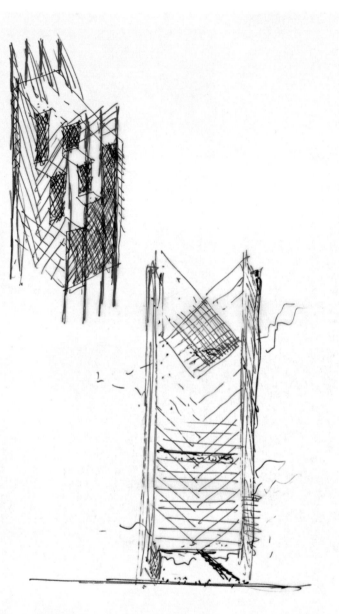

Foster won a competition to replace the bank's old headquarters, built in 1936. The site faces north, toward mainland China, and also overlooks Statue Square and the harbor. Foster's building is magnificent and majestic, but it was initially criticized by Hong Kong residents because of its indifference to the rules of *feng shui*, the Chinese system of harmonizing oneself physically with the natural universe. (Among other defects, the building arrested the paths of dragons coming down from the mountain to drink from the bay.) As a matter of fact, Foster's buildings often reveal a deeper interest in themselves than in the rest of the world; their exploration of their own internal possibilities, and of the possibilities of technology, is often a stronger motive in the design than any concern for the building's site or for the local culture. It is through this single-mindedness, on the other hand, that Foster's work has advanced architecture. His contributions to the built world—whether in London, Tokyo, or Hong Kong—have sometimes made earthly cities more interesting than science fiction.

—Paola Antonelli

Mario Botta

Row Housing Project, Pregassona, Switzerland

Elevation. Project: 1985–86. Drawing: 1985. Color pencil and graphite on diazotype, 20¾ × 53¼" (52.7 × 135.3 cm). Gift of the architect, 1987

Leon Krier

**The Completion of Washington, D.C., Project:
The National Gallery; The National Pantheon;
The Grand Canal; The Mall**

Perspective. 1985. Ink and graphite on paper, 11⅞ × 15⅝" (30.2 × 39.7 cm).
Purchase, 1985

O.M.A. (Office for Metropolitan Architecture) (Rem Koolhaas, Götz Keller, Willem-Jan Neutelings with Brigitte Kochta, Marty Kohn, Luc Reuse, Ron Steiner, Jeroen Thomas, Garciella Torre)

The Hague City Hall Project, The Hague, The Netherlands

Exterior perspective. Project: 1986. Drawing: 1987. Pastel and graphite on paper, 62" × 6'9" (157.5 × 205.7 cm). Drawing attributed to Luc Reuse. Purchase, 1992

Tadao Ando

Chikatsu-Asuka Historical Museum, Minami-Kawachi, Osaka, Japan

Exterior perspective. Project: 1989–91. Drawing: c. 1989–91. Graphite and crayon with scoring on paper, 11⅝ × 33⅛" (29.5 × 84.2 cm). Gift of the architect, 1993

The Chikatsu-Asuka Historical Museum, Osaka, designed by Tadao Ando, is dedicated to exhibiting and researching artifacts of the Kofun and Asuka periods of Japanese culture, from the fourth to the seventh century A.D. The museum is located in a region containing over 200 burial mounds, or *kofun*, from that era, and there are a number of archaeological sites in the building's immediate neighborhood, which has been designated a historical park. As far as possible, then, Ando's design preserves the park's topography, altering it minimally through the use of architectural elements that serve more than one function: the building's roof doubles as sets of stairs leading up to an observation tower and plaza, together constituting stepped viewing platforms from which to look at the tombs in their natural surroundings. The concept focuses, Ando has said, "on architecture's power to produce a new landscape": like a large berm, the museum becomes an integral part of the landscape that the museum also serves to exhibit.

Inside the building, objects excavated from the burial mounds are exhibited in a darkened interior, evoking the interiors of the tombs in which they were discovered. Ando's use of concrete as a construction material recalls the work of Le Corbusier and Louis Kahn, his architectural mentors, yet he combines this preference with a Japanese aesthetic of contrast—light and dark, interior and exterior, enclosed and expansive, hard and soft, nature and city, east and west. The subtle interplay of these opposites in Ando's buildings produces rich environments, and some of this is captured in the drawing: the hard-edged graphite lines marking the imposed, man-made structure offer a counterpoint to the softer shades of color depicting the enveloping landscape that Ando seeks to echo.

—**Matilda McQuaid**

Santiago Calatrava
Lyons Airport Railroad Station, Lyons-Satolas, France

Plan and elevation. Project: 1989–94. Drawing: 1992. Crayon and graphite on tracing paper, 28½ × 36" (72.4 × 91.4 cm). Gift of the architect, 1996

Elizabeth Diller and Ricardo Scofidio (Diller and Scofidio)

Slow House, North Haven, New York

Plan of lower level and sections. Project: 1988–90. Drawing: 1989.
Electronic print on frosted polymer sheet with graphite and color ink
mounted on painted wood with metal, 47⅝ × 36½ × 1½" (121 × 92.7 ×
3.8 cm). Partially built. Marshall Cogan Purchase Fund and Jeffrey P. Klein
Purchase Fund, 1992

Elizabeth Diller and Ricardo Scofidio's Slow House is an oceanfront vacation home designed for an art collector and entrepreneur. The project explores the idea of the vacation house as a place offering both an escape from a fast-paced urban environment and the ability to reconnect with the city at any time; in the drawing opposite, in fact, a series of transverse sections extending from a plan of the lower level trace the path from the city to the house, with its cherished ocean view. (Challenging the conventions of architectural representation, Diller and Scofidio have executed this drawing on a sheet of vellum mounted on a wooden board, leaving drawing equipment attached to the final product.) The split passage between the first and the second levels, the curved plan, and the torqued outer wall of the house thwart direct visual access to this view, at the structure's southwest end, "slowing" the visitor's approach to it. The architects have explained that the house "is conceived as a passage, a door that leads to a window . . . a physical entry to an optical departure."

Collaborators since 1979, Diller and Scofidio have made the relationship between architecture and technology a pervasive theme in their work. The collage drawing *TV in Picture Window*

Apparatus shows them manipulating a view of the ocean through the frame of a picture window and the technology of a video camera and monitor. Rather than the view itself, the *representation* of the view becomes their primary interest; indeed the monitor obstructs the actual view, while the camera transmits a copy of the view to the screen. Thus the drawing represents three different types of view, real, framed, and virtual, using a different medium for each one: a cutout magazine reproduction is pasted onto a pencil drawing of a plan and partial interior elevation of the picture window. Color photocopies of exterior perspectives, located beneath a Mylar sheet that covers the entire drawing, tie the parts of the image together. The right side of the drawing, a study of the mechanisms of the monitor's support arm, illustrates how the inhabitant can control the location of the television image.

—Melanie Domino

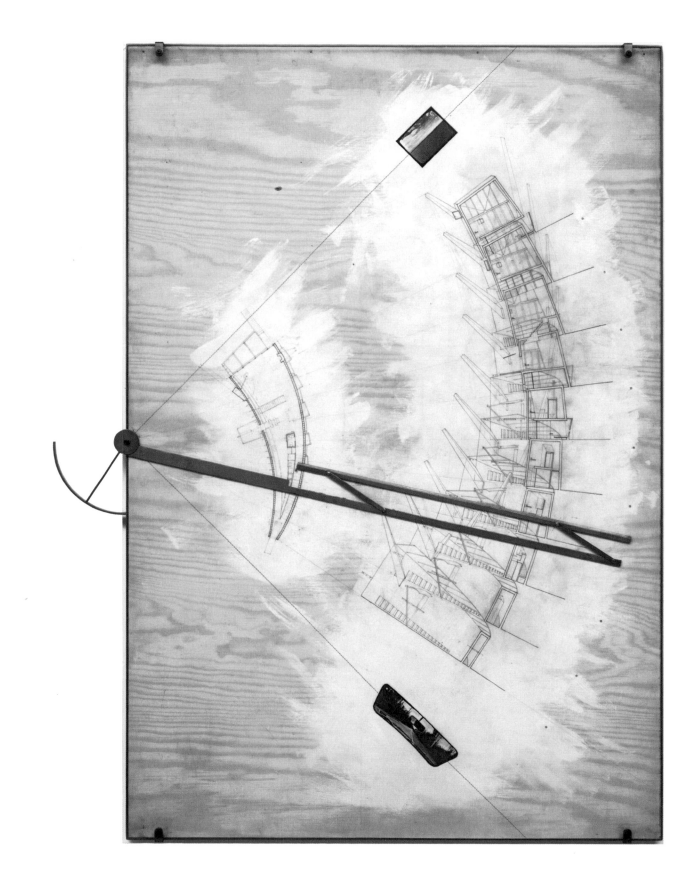

Elizabeth Diller and Ricardo Scofidio (Diller and Scofidio)

TV in Picture Window Apparatus, Slow House, North Haven, New York

Perspective and plans. Project: 1988–90. Drawing: 1991. Cut-and-pasted color photocopy and graphite on frosted polymer sheet taped to board with cut-and-pasted color photography, 12⅜ × 18⅜" (31.4 × 46.7 cm). Partially built. Gift of the architects in honor of Lily Auchincloss, 1994

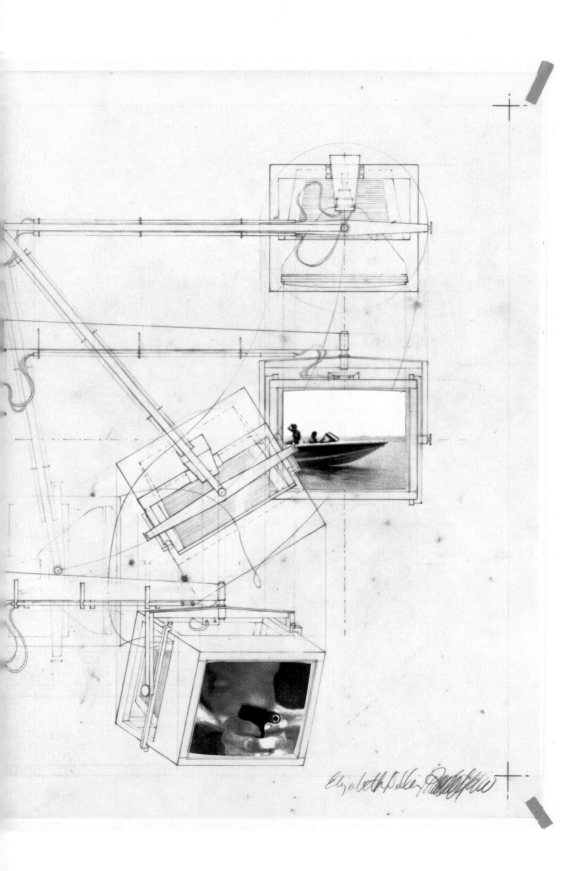

Thom Mayne with Andrew Zago
Sixth Street House Project, Santa Monica, California

Isometrics and plan. Project: 1986–87. Drawing: 1990. Screenprint with metal foil on paper, 40 × 30" (101.6 × 76.2 cm). Delineators: Thom Mayne with Selwyn Tings. Printmaker: John Nichols. Edition: 41/50. A revised version of the Sixth Street House was eventually built in 1997. Given anonymously, 1999

Thom Mayne's drawing for the Sixth Street House invokes architectural conventions only to surpass their limitations. By collapsing plan, elevation, and detail through juxtapositions of scale, obliquity, projection, and rotation, Mayne challenges the historical view of drawing as a passive medium at the service of architecture.

Mayne's design involves inserting eleven found machinery parts into a shell wrapping a preexisting bungalow (his own). Reworked into functional elements—staircase, fireplace, shower—these parts, Mayne claims, would bring invention to the site and have "the capacity to embody in built form an imagined prehistory of a place, a contemporary archaeology (past and future) and its subsequent transmission across time." This drawing, which layers a 1:24 detail and a 1:16 elevation or section over a 1:16 plan, functions similarly. The steel parts—represented by cutouts of metallic foil—appear as if unearthed, pulled out one by one, rotated, examined, and set aside, leaving behind the gray traces of their impression. Reassembled like cogs in a wheel, they become constructions of reinvented form.

Mayne is a founding member of both the Santa Monica architectural firm Morphosis and the Southern California Institute of Architecture. His work recalls the machine aesthetic of the early-twentieth-century avant-garde and the archaeological and genealogical methods of Michel Foucault. Originally conceived as the terminus of his investigation—that is, as architecture—Mayne's drawings mimic the parts (found objects) that he reappropriates—each of them, as Mayne says, something "simultaneously 'a part of' its context . . . while isolated, detached, disquieting, critical, and untrustful of the world 'as it exists.'"

—Tina di Carlo

41/50

Neil Denari

Prototype Architecture School No. 5 Project, Los Angeles, California

Elevations. 1992. Ink, airbrush, and cut-and-pasted printed self-adhesive polymer sheet on frosted polymer sheet, 24½ × 33¹/₁₆" (62.2 × 84 cm). Ralph Fehlbaum Purchase Fund, 1998

These elevations of Neil Denari's Prototype Architecture School No. 5 are emblematic of the singular language of design and graphic expression that Denari has developed since establishing his office, COR-TEX, in New York in 1986. Designed for a site on Wilshire Boulevard, Los Angeles (the city to which COR-TEX relocated in 1988), the school project is one of a number of important theoretical works, including several competition entries, that Denari undertook in the 1990s. The building embraces a frank functional expressivity. Each space assumes an optimized shape, creating an architectural body whose organs are clearly identifiable.

Devoid of what may be called natural life—human figures or greenery—Denari's drawings portray a highly technological vision of architecture. Their airbrushed inks and Pantone colors are as cool as the metallic surfaces they portray. A rationalized vocabulary defines the two-dimensional space of the drawing as well:

gridded backgrounds, metric devices, and other drafting conventions, many of them rather arcane to the casual viewer, create a dense text, a techno-incunabulum. Ironically, this visual lexicon is produced not by machine but by hand, and laboriously. Nor can the drawings be considered truly objective: the heavy shadowing and stark surfaces suggest both the anxiety and the euphoria of the twentieth century's love of the machine—a love-hate relationship certainly still evident in the cyberworld we inhabit today. Denari's project portrays the moment when the two worlds merge. In Italo Calvino's words, "The iron machines still exist, but they obey the orders of weightless bits."

—Terence Riley

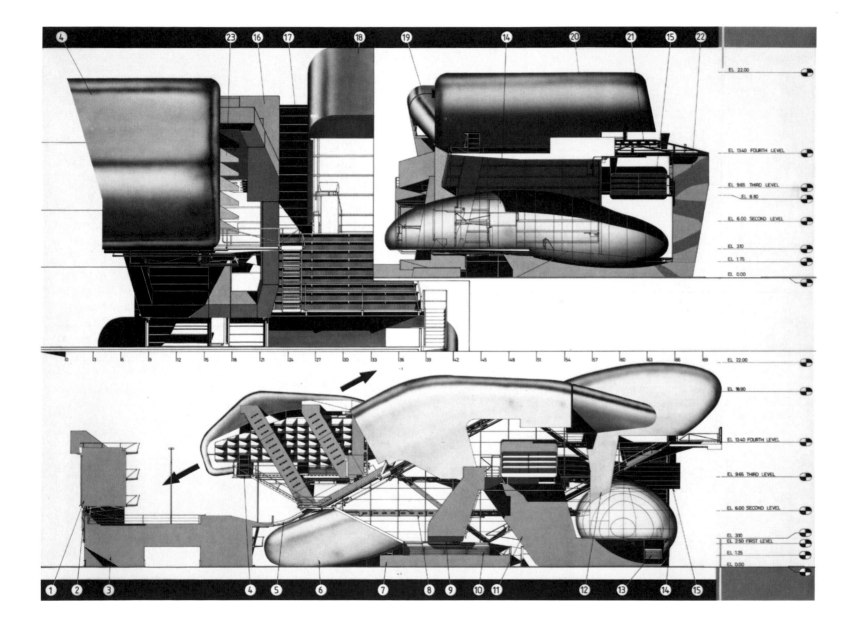

Frank O. Gehry

University of Toledo Center for the Visual Arts, Toledo, Ohio

Exterior perspective. Project: 1990–92. Drawing: 1990. Ink on paper, 9 × 12″
(22.9 × 30.5 cm). Gift of the architect in honor of Lily Auchincloss, 1994

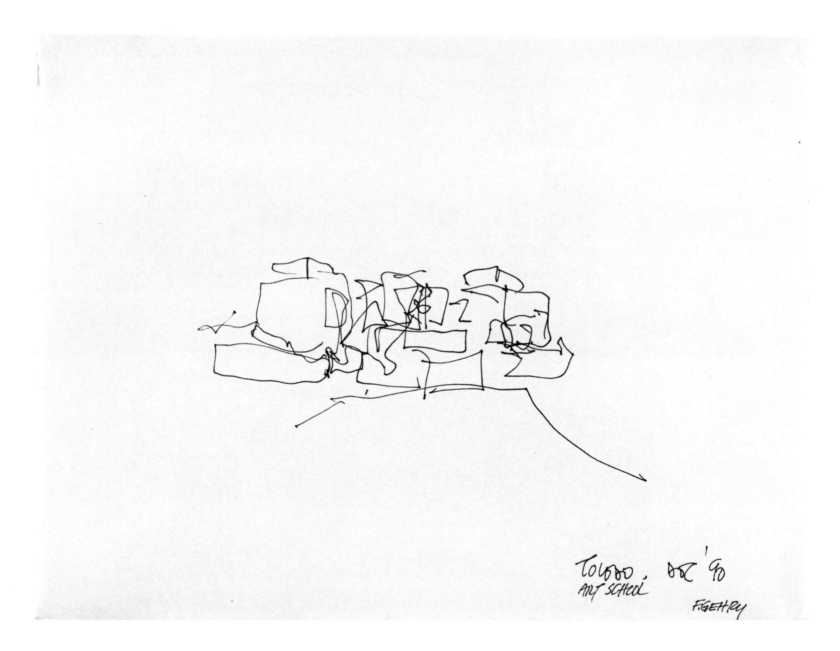

Rafael Viñoly
Tokyo International Forum, Tokyo, Japan

Exterior perspectives. Project: 1989–96. Drawing: 1991. Crayon on six sheets of paper, each sheet 11½ × 8" (29.2 × 20.3 cm). Gift of the architect, 1993

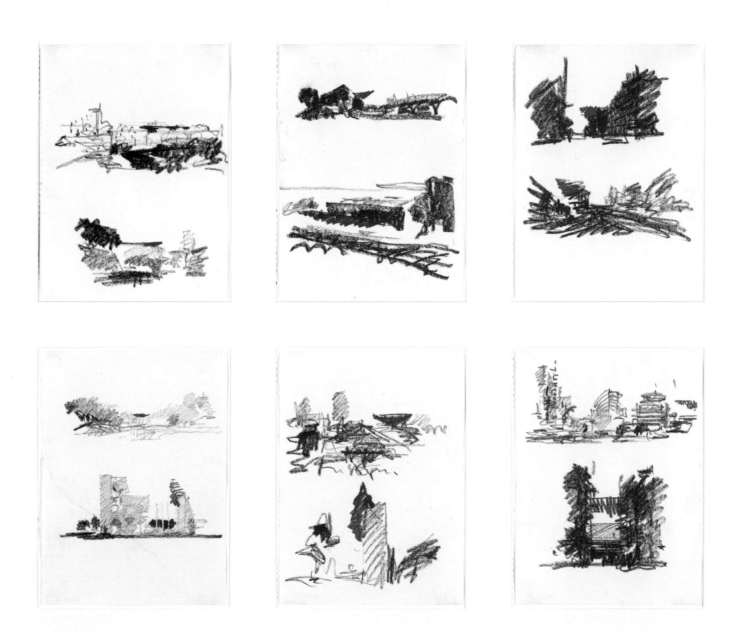

Arata Isozaki

Nara Convention Hall, Nara, Japan

Perspective sketches for plaza and entrance lobby. Project: 1992–98.
Drawing: 1992. Color ink on tracing paper, 12 × 19⅝" (30.5 × 49.9 cm).
Gift of the architect, 1993

Nara Convention Hall, Nara, Japan

Exterior perspective. Project: 1992–98. Drawing: 1992. Acrylic on
computer-generated print, 21¾ × 37¼" (55.2 × 94.6 cm). Gift of the
architect, 1993

Arata Isozaki's design for the Nara Convention Hall was the winning entry in an international competition in 1992. The program required three principal spaces, respectively accommodating 100, 500, and 2,000 people, and all flexible enough to serve multiple purposes, from concerts to conventions. The hall was to be the centerpiece of a series of structures planned for the city and prefecture of Nara, the master plan for which was drawn up by Kisho Kurokawa.

Isozaki's main structure takes the form of a gigantic ellipse that extends the length of the site. In the sketch plan the ellipse is first set along the axis of the city's preexisting grid, then is rotated twenty-three degrees, forming an entrance hall parallel to an adjacent railway station. The sculptural form tapers gently toward the roof (a vast field of glass-tube solar collectors). Though the form of the building is abstract, its curving profile and ponderous presence relate to the monumental roof forms of Nara's most notable monument, the Todaiji Temple, constructed in 734 A.D. Its exterior skin, sheathed in zinc and gray-ceramic tile, also recalls the dull luster of the traditional gray *ibushi*-style roofs of Todaiji and other important temple structures.

The sketch and the computer-generated drawing, both of which appeared in an exhibition at The Museum of Modern Art in 1992–93, together show the full range of graphic techniques available to Isozaki at the time. The sketch portrays the signature dimension of architectural design in its most generative form; the computer drawing is less personal, depicting not the act of generation but the end result of a long design process. Its cool tones and even surface render the qualities of the ceramic-tile skin, and provided a visual understanding of the total design well before construction was to begin.

—Terence Riley

Chuck Hoberman
Iris Dome Project

Interior perspective. Project: 1990–93. Drawing: 1994. Computer-generated print, 31½ × 43½" (80 × 110.5 cm). Gift of the architect in honor of Lily Auchincloss, 1994

Lauretta Vinciarelli

Orange Sound Project

1999. Watercolor, graphite, and color ink on paper, 30 × 22"
(76.2 × 55.9 cm). Mrs. Gianluigi Gabetti Purchase Fund, 2000

Orange Sound Project

1999. Watercolor, graphite, and color ink on paper, 30 × 22" (76.2 ×
55.9 cm). Mrs. Gianluigi Gabetti Purchase Fund, 2000

Orange Sound Project

1999. Watercolor, graphite, and color ink on paper, 30 × 22" (76.2 ×
55.9 cm). Mrs. Gianluigi Gabetti Purchase Fund, 2000

The extraordinary luminous watercolors that constitute the Orange Sound series are visual poems that give shape to what is formless: light and water. Although Lauretta Vinciarelli trained as an architect, her imaginary universe respects no program, function, or client. We view spaces that do not exist, except on paper, where an invisible light source creates the illusion of placid reflections on a changing volume of water contained in a vessel or anonymous architectural structure. In Vinciarelli's virtuoso handling, the transparent, glowing quality of the watercolor medium conveys transcendent feelings. Void of extraneous details such as ordinary things, human presence, and recognizable architectural elements and signs, the compositions assume metaphysical qualities.

The lateral symmetry in each work provides a sense of calm balance and control (Vinciarelli suggests it provides a "system of rules") that serves as a connective thread between each drawing in the series. This seriality suggests narrative, and the drawings are numbered one through seven, but the sequence is somewhat random; Vinciarelli has likened it to the notes of a musical scale, but just as the notes in a scale are played in different orders to create musical passages, the drawings too can be viewed in varying sequences. In whatever order they appear, the changing tonal variations from one drawing to the next—the shifting qualities of light and shadow in the spaces, on the surfaces, and on the changing volumes of water, with their mesmerizing reflections—will stimulate feelings and imply a fluid narrative.

The warm orange and ocher tones of Orange Sound recall remembered landscapes, perhaps particularly the American Southwest, where Vinciarelli spent time with the artist Donald Judd. She clearly admires Judd's serial Minimalist sculpture, and art in a similar vein. Throughout her work, which exists primarily on paper, Vinciarelli has pushed the traditional boundaries between art and architecture by exploring the relationship between the two disciplines. Her abiding interest in formal typologies, and her investigations of the essentially immeasurable qualities of light, space, and reflection, suggest both a realm of the sublime and a place where meaningful architecture can begin.

—Peter Reed

Index of Plates

Photograph Credits

P. 10: Avery Architectural and Fine Arts Library, Columbia University in the City of New York

P. 18: The Museum of Modern Art, New York. Photograph: Jacek Marczewski

P. 20: The Museum of Modern Art, New York. Photograph: Geo H. Van Anda

P. 21, above right: The Museum of Modern Art, New York. Photograph: Jacek Marczewski. Below left: both The Museum of Modern Art, New York

P. 23: The Museum of Modern Art, New York. Photograph: Soichi Sunami

P. 24: The Museum of Modern Art, New York. Photograph: Soichi Sunami

P. 25: The Museum of Modern Art, New York.

P. 27: The Museum of Modern Art, New York. Photograph: George Barrows

P. 28: The Museum of Modern Art, New York. Photograph: Jacek Marczewski

P. 29: The Museum of Modern Art, New York. Photograph: George Barrows

P. 30, left: The Museum of Modern Art, New York. Photograph: Soichi Sunami. Right: The Museum of Modern Art, New York. Photograph: Mali Olatunji

P. 31, above: The Museum of Modern Art, New York. Photograph: George Cserna. Below: The Museum of Modern Art, New York. Photograph: David Allison

P. 32: The Museum of Modern Art, New York. Photograph: Kate Keller

P. 33, above left: The Museum of Modern Art, New York. Photograph: Albert Fenn. Below left: Ezra Stoller © Esto. Below right: The Museum of Modern Art, New York. Photograph: Kate Keller

P. 34: The Museum of Modern Art, New York. Photograph: Kate Keller

P. 35: The Museum of Modern Art, New York. Photograph: Mali Olatunji

P. 36: The Museum of Modern Art, New York. Photograph: Mali Olatunji

All plates The Museum of Modern Art, New York, photographs by Jacek Marczewski, except pp. 71, 219, 235: Tom Griesel. Pp. 60–61, 67, 98, 103, 140: Kate Keller. Pp. 92, 93: Kate Keller and Mali Olatunji. P. 57: The Museum of Modern Art, New York